the

I AM

Meditations

365 Affirmative Prayer Treatments/Meditations
on Inner Peace, Grace and Joy.

JACOB GLASS

DEDICATION TO THREE ANGELS:

Richard W. Becker
Karl Shafer
Beverly Hutchinson McNeff

INTRODUCTION

You're a smart person. You don't need me to explain to you how to use a book of 365 Meditations/Affirmative Prayer Treatments. It's yours. Use it any way that you find helpful. You can even tear out the pages and paste them on the fridge if it helps.

I do have some suggestions to try though. I designed it with the idea that it be read as early in the day as possible to set the tone for your day. Ideally, you could read it and then sit and let the words sink in, meditate or contemplate them. In fact, you can change any words the feel more "right" for you. I also suggest slowly reading it out loud. It makes a difference. You can even write it out yourself to let it sink into your subconscious more deeply.

You can read one page a day for a year and beyond. You can stay on a Treatment for multiple days if you like. You can read it in order, or you can plop it open to any page and use that as your Treatment for the day. It's your book now. However you use it will be the right way for you. The main thing is not to put it up on a shelf- USE IT and watch the miracles unfold in your world.

May this book bless you and enrich your daily life. I send you love and Light on your journey.

p.s. This book is self-published. Please excuse any typographical or gramatical errors that you may find. Try to focus on the content rather than the form. Thank you so much.

EPIGRAPH

"Each day should be devoted to miracles. The purpose of time is to enable you to learn how to use time constructively. It is thus a teaching device and a means to an end. Time will cease when it is no longer useful in facilitating learning."

A Course in Miracles

"Each day bears watching. Your moods need your scrutiny. Your ideas should be selected as wisely as you would choose a diamond."

Raymond Charles Barker

ACKNOWLEDGMENTS

Thank you Brother Jesus for bringing this book through. A special thank you to Julie Westerfield for asking me to do this book and encouraging me along the way.

THE I AM MEDITATIONS

Affirmative Prayer Treatment 1

God is with me now – I am not alone nor separate.

There is a Divine Plan for my life which is now unfolding.

Today I walk in Grace to my greater good.

I see all around me opportunities to bless & be blessed.

I give my hands, voice and feet to God to guide today.

I am the Light of the world and I go forth happily

to shine on those who cross my mind or path.

This is a day of miracles and light.

I am happy to be alive.

Affirmative Prayer Treatment 2

Today I am awakening to the Great Rays infusing me

with Wisdom, Guidance and Grace in all things.

This is a day of joyful ease as I open to receive rather

than to conquer, control or get. Instead, I allow and accept.

Invisible hands reach out to guide and direct me.

Opportunities present themselves in perfect timing & ways.

My thoughts turn in gentle happy directions.

AFFIRMATIVE PRAYER TREATMENT 3

The Universe is friendly and loving.

My world is happy and Life is good.

As I align myself with Spirit,

miracles light the path before me

and I walk one Graceful step at a time.

I forgive the past and release all grievances as

I focus my attention on all the gifts of today.

I am filled with the Light of the Great Rays

which illumine my world and draw to me all

that is for the highest good of all concerned.

Affirmative Prayer Treatment 4

I am living by Grace and sourced by Love.

I have dissolved all concepts of struggle and suffering.

I invoke the energy of the Cosmos as

I call my good to me today.

The limitless abundance of the Universe is flowing now

and I am an open available vessel, ready to be filled.

There is no need to worry or rush – perfect flow is mine.

Problems solve themselves & dissolve before they appear.

Answers to my requests come with ease and perfect timing.

Healing Light surrounds me & flows through me.

The air is thick with miracles & joyful transformations.

My heart is open – my mind is clear and spacious.

Today I look through eyes of love

at a world of effortless Grace.

<u>AFFIRMATIVE PRAYER TREATMENT 5</u>

I greet this day with Peace, Joy and Love Divine.

Before me miracles are lighting the way to the open doors

which lead to my greatest good so far.

I give my full attention to the good, the true and the Holy.

My mind is focused on appreciation, praise and gratitude

as I give myself over to the effortless joyful Grace of God.

I am enjoying my NOW and happy to see what is next!

AFFIRMATIVE PRAYER TREATMENT 6

Life responds quickly to my positive thoughts today.

I am love and I see love all around me as

I walk the path of Grace and gently unfolding good.

I release all fear and resistance and

I trust Life to guide and direct my day with joyful ease.

I cannot fail to be at the right place at the right time.

All that I do is blessed, multiplied and prospered today and

the Universe can arrange every detail with great ease.

I am happy, grateful and filled with radiant faith in Life!

AFFIRMATIVE PRAYER TREATMENT 7

I am Springing forward into love and appreciation
as I gently release old limiting thoughts & beliefs.
I am giving my full attention to all the good in my world.
I surrender into Divine Grace and walk in Love today.
All fear and worry are dissolved in this Love and Grace.
I have a wonderful mind which keeps track of my good
and keeps me happily on the highlighted route.
I have a wonderful heart full of love and appreciation.
I greet this day with all the joy and love in my heart
and Life greets me by reflecting that same joy & love.
I relax into my world of ever-increasing Light.

AFFIRMATIVE PRAYER TREATMENT 8

Today I marinate in gratitude and quiet appreciation.

My soul is touching the Universal Soul today

as I walk in Grace.

Infinite Wisdom guides my thoughts and actions today

as I remember that miracles are everyday things

for anyone with Vision.

I know that right here, right now, all things are held

perfectly in the hands of God and that whatever I need to

know is revealed to me as I RELAX and

trust in the still small Voice within me.

I offer myself to be joyfully used by Life today –

to be truly Helpful.

I release all resistance and judgment as

I see only the love and goodness in

all those who appear in my world today.

Where I am, all is well.

Let the miracles begin!

AFFIRMATION PRAYER TREATMENT 9

There is a Dynamic Power and Presence in the Universe

that I call God.

God is good, Life is good – and I am good.

I am not weak, nor damaged, not insane, nor a sinner.

I am capable and powerful. I am a Child of the God of Love.

All things are possible for me and I create

a wonderful life for myself through

this Divine Love within me.

My heart is full of overflowing Love for all of Life.

Love is everywhere and I am lovable and loving.

Today I am channeling this Love, therefore my Presence is

healing, soothing, uplifting and joyful to those around me.

Today is a delightful day of unfolding good.

Affirmative Prayer Treatment 10

I am open to experiencing the best of everything.

Nothing is too good for me – nothing too good to be true.

Life loves me and wants to express AS a thriving me.

This is a lavish abundant limitless Universe – there is more

than enough good to go around – so many opportunities for

good, so much money, so many single available people,

good food, knowledge, love, kindness, resources, ideas,

homes, healings and healers, talent, understanding,

inspiration, support and good connections.

There is no limitation, no ceiling to what I can

be, do, have or experience.

I am lining up with my greater good as I give thanks

for all that has already been given and received.

I am happy in my now and joyfully open to even more good.

Today I am focused on the opportunities to up my vibration.

I am tuned into the Guidance that

leads me to the open doors!

AFFIRMATION PRAYER TREATMENT 11

There is a Power and a Presence guiding my day.

This Presence only loves and knows nothing of limitation.

In It I live and move and have my Being.

I relax into the Everlasting Arms today and

allow my good to flow freely and abundantly.

I need do nothing but believe, trust and know this Truth

and follow the Guidance given on where to go,

what to do or say.

There is no one to impress – nothing to compete for.

There is more than enough good for

all to thrive in the Light.

I open to receive the gifts of God today as Life unfolds

a day of perfect order, beauty and all that is good.

I am blessed and I am a blessing.

All is well.

AFFIRMATION 12

I am living in a Spiritual Universe,

formed from loving Thought.

My thought is creative and is creating my world today.

Today I choose grateful, joyous, and loving thoughts as

I know that these thoughts will be reflected back to me.

I do not have to design the ways and means for this is an

Intelligent Universe that knows HOW and when and where.

My part is to align myself with my greater good as I RELAX

and allow in calm expectancy –

my heart and mind open and receptive.

This is a day of divine fulfillment and

limitless possibilities for good.

I happily participate as I allow my Creative Imagination

to vision only the best knowing there

is no need to worry or rush.

The Universe has perfect timing and

knows where to find me.

My faith and belief in the good are

growing and expanding daily.

There is no opposite to this Divine Power and Presence.

All is well in me and in my world.

<u>Affirmative Prayer Treatment 13</u>

Nothing can hinder nor obstruct

my good today except a thought.

I now dissolve all limiting beliefs and ideas, knowing that

I live in a lavishly abundant Universe of endless possibilities.

I stretch out my arms and open my heart today to receive.

The Creative Force of Life is now flowing through me and

everything I need to know is revealed to me as

as I align myself with this Creative Intelligence.

My thoughts are creative and

my words are containers for Power.

I think and speak my world into being today and

I expect a day of peace, joy and ease as

I relax into the Power that effortlessly creates galaxies

Affirmative Prayer Treatment 14

Today I leave my littleness behind as

I make the choices that bring the Greater Life

into my Consciousness and into my experience.

My thoughts today are Guided by the Council of Light

within my own Consciousness, where Truth abides.

All that I do today is infused with the Love and Grace

which blesses the giver and the receiver alike.

I open my arms to welcome the gifts of Life today

as I remember that God's Will for me is perfect happiness.

I am never selling God on my good ideas

or trying to win favor.

All favor is already mine as I step up my capacity to let it in.

Nothing hinders or delays my good – I am gratefully ready.

I release all mistakes, guilt and shame from the past as

I step into my Great and Glorious Present today.

AFFIRMATIVE PRAYER TREATMENT 15

Here in my own yard, all is well.

I stay in my own business and clean up my own vibration

by choosing the thoughts that feel good when I think them.

There is a Power and a Presence which guides my actions

and leads my feet as I align myself with Higher Thoughts.

There is no need to struggle or strive to get somewhere.

I am following my joy and peace through the open doors.

I am anointed with Grace to accomplish all with ease as

I relax into the downstream thoughts,

knowing that all is well.

Affirmative Prayer Treatment 16

I AM waking up to myself more each day.

In this Holy Week I AM giving birth to my true Self

as I release all that no longer serves me and

open up to all the gifts of the Universe –

my arms open wide.

The more good I allow in my life, the more

I have to share and to spare with my sisters and brothers.

I AM a Divine Center of loving abundance.

I boldly and gratefully embrace this new day knowing that

Life loves me and that everything I need is here and now.

AFFIRMATIVE PRAYER TREATMENT 17

I rise up in JOY today as I allow the Light of the Season

to fill me up and flood out of me in

waves of great abundance.

My hands, feet and voice are joyfully used to Help and Heal.

There is nothing the Light within me cannot accomplish

as I step back and allow the

Christ Consciousness to lead the way.

My part is to do MY part and to release

all that is beyond my control.

I put one foot in front of the other as I breathe in Peace and

Grace to light my journey through the world,

blessing all as I go.

This is a day of Divine Fulfillment and of elegant miracles.

Affirmative Prayer Treatment 18

I am blessed and I am a blessing.

My world is filled with the most wonderful people

and we are co-creating a life of joyful abundant good today.

All are held in Holy Light today as

the doors of plenty open wide.

Divine Order is established in my affairs and

all unfolds in great peaceful ease as I relax and breathe.

I am well loved and well able to give abundant love

as my heart opens wide to all who want to joyfully play.

Divine Love now draws to me all that is needed for my

greatest happiness and complete satisfaction today.

Nothing good is denied me and I open to receive

all the good that is mine today.

I am a grateful part of the Divine All.

A<small>FFIRMATIVE</small> P<small>RAYER</small> T<small>REATMENT</small> 19

Life is to be savored and enjoyed!

I am lining up with my highest good

and adjusting my attitude as I tune to JOY.

I allow happy experiences to flow on my path

this week as I focus on laughing away all fear

thoughts while I walk with ease through the open doors.

AFFIRMATIVE PRAYER TREATMENT 20

If I am sad, if I am hurt, if I am lonely or in despair,

if I forget Who I am, or am filled with shame or regret,

if I am lost or overwhelmed and confused, if I lose my way,

if I feel sick, or wounded, or gripped by fear, if I feel

abandoned, weak, deprived or that I am not enough,

if I feel that I cannot go on, or do not know which way to

turn —I do not need to withdraw from the world to hide

from life. I can turn to my Refuge and Security by hanging

on the Vine as I drink in the golden elixir of the Divine Love

that nourishes me back to wholeness

and to remembrance of the Truth.

The Angels encircle me while I am being restored and

renewed even as I go about my normal day of

people, places and things.

Grace enfolds me and I relax into the Everlasting Arms of

the Love that forgives, heals, soothes and feeds my soul.

I let go of time as I allow my heart to open to RECEIVE all

of the healing Qi that is flowing through me now.

There is no hurry, no way to rush the seasons of life.

Where I am is where I am, and I allow myself this time.

Mercy, kindness, gentleness and peace are the sun

that warm me now as I hang on the Vine

drinking in the One Power and Presence

which restoreth my soul.

AFFIRMATIVE PRAYER TREATMENT 21

I am running my own race today. There is no competition, condemnation nor criticism in me nor towards me. Everyone wins in my space, including me. I do not bother with the ego notion of dreaming big, for I dream JOYFULLY instead. In Spirit, there is no size, no comparison, no order of difficulty. There is nothing to prove, no one to impress. I release all desire to be special, for God created me and there is nothing I need add to make myself more valuable. I am happily playing in my own yard.

I now give 100% of my attention to those who love, adore and support me just as I am. I only spend time with those it feels great to be around. I withdraw all attention from those who don't get me, don't like me, don't approve of me, or want me to be different. I release them with love and turn entirely away from them and I now only attract and spend time where there is mutual love, support and great joy. There is no one and nothing to audition for – I've got the part of ME and I am playing it with great ease and joy as I savor all my own unique weirdness here in the world I have created in the Possibility Matrix.

Affirmative Prayer Treatment 22

I need DO nothing for I live and walk in the Christ Consciousness today. There is no separation and no lack of any good in my world. I will not worry or fret – I will not let ego steal my joy. The creation of this day is not based on my doing, but on my Consciousness and Who I choose as my Guide for the day.

I choose Spirit within to lean on and walk with through my day. I am shown the good, the beautiful and the holy as I allow my mind to be healed of all attack thoughts.

As I relax into the Grace of God, all my good comes rushing to meet me, solutions unfold in ease, and problems are solved before they can take root.

I breathe in the Peace of God and this vibration of Peace emanates from me and touches all those who are open to receive it. There is nothing for me to struggle with or against, nothing to strive after nor yearn for. As I rest in God, I remember that truly, I need do nothing but follow my Joy, Peace and Love as it calls me together with the greater good of all concerned.

AFFIRMATIVE PRAYER TREATMENT 23

I live in a Friendly Universe which responds to my vibration.

My thoughts, words, attitudes and actions

are the seeds I sow.

I will harvest in abundance just what I plant,

nothing more or less than that.

I choose today to sow seeds of joy, kindness,

love and abundance.

I sow laughter, vitality, warmth, goodness and mercy.

There is nothing for me to get –

I merely harvest my own crops.

I release all struggle, striving, manipulation and control.

I trust the Universe today to respond to my loving energy

as I walk in Grace and peace, sharing my Light with

those who are open to receive it.

All is well in me and in my world for this is

a day of Divine Harvest and Happy Sowing.

<u>Affirmative Prayer Treatment 24</u>

I walk in gentle peace and gratitude today.

There is nothing for me to fight against,

nothing for me to strive after or to manipulate.

I align myself with the heartbeat of the Great Mother Tao

and allow myself to be carried downstream.

I place the past, present and future in Her hands

as I breathe in love and breathe out kindness.

Goodness and mercy shall follow me all the days of my life

as I release everyone into Divine Care and

entrust them to God's ministering Angels.

Today, miracles light my way on

the gentle pathways of peace.

May I be joyfully used by Love to brighten the world

as I surrender into Love, Joy, Peace and Grace.

AFFIRMATIVE PRAYER TREATMENT 25

Today I forgive and I am forgiven.

I surrender to Spirit all shame, blame and guilt.

I am washed clean in the Living Waters as

I focus on the good in all creatures.

My mistakes do not define me.

I have a chance today to begin again.

I will not punish myself nor anyone else.

By the Grace of God, this is a day of renewal as

I release all attack thoughts &

replace them with gentle love.

I am guided by Spirit to make good choices

and I turn to the Presence within to meet all my needs.

I am happy and free in the Peace of God today.

.

AFFIRMATIVE PRAYER TREATMENT 26

I am magnetic to my good!

There is a Dynamic Something in the Universe which

responds to my thoughts, words, feelings and attitudes.

Today, I choose to focus on all that is good as

I go on rampages of appreciation and praise.

I TELL people how wonderful they are as

I lift them up – and I tell myself how wonderful I am

as I am lifted up to higher and higher levels of Joy!

I am irresistible to my greater good and

I am gathering up evidence that Life loves me.

My Infinite Source is within me and the blessings are

springing forth from me today in all directions.

I am not worried about the future for

the best is yet to come as I envision only the good.

There is no need for me to make anything happen nor

to be aggressive or pushy, for miracles of love

are opening the doors to my good with Grace and ease.

I remain calm and yet alert as I bless the world and

count up my own blessings while walking this path of Peace.

AFFIRMATIVE PRAYER TREATMENT 27

Love makes my world beautiful today.

As I look through the eyes of love today,

I see a world of beauty and of Light.

I will not focus on the errors in myself or others,

but instead will be a detective seeking clues

leading to the innocence, kindness and Grace in us all.

I am shredding all evidence to the contrary as

I dissolve all walls around my heart

and take down all defenses.

Love is my strength today as I open my heart

to receive the Love of God & let it flow through me

to the world around me.

A<small>FFIRMATIVE</small> P<small>RAYER</small> T<small>REATMENT</small> 28

This is a day of meditation and stillness for me
even as I go about the world living my normal life.
I take my eyes off the bigger picture and focus on each
small sacred step as a holy action infused
with love, love, love.
I devote today to serving the Spirit of Love as It uses
my hands, feet and voice to channel Love and Peace
through me even in the most mundane
of errands and happenings.

I allow the small "me" to dissolve as I step back and let
Him lead the way, for I am walking in Grace today.
This is a day of beauty and of Light as all that is not Love
dissolves away from my Being and I am restored to peace.

AFFIRMATIVE PRAYER TREATMENT 29

I do not have to believe every thought

that comes into mind.

I have the freedom to choose today what thoughts

to keep and what thoughts to dissolve back

into the ethers through surrender.

Today, I choose the feelings I want to feel and the dominant

thoughts I want to think about myself, life and each

experience before me.

What a glorious world in which I am not

at the whim of my moods.

Today, I choose the peace, love and joy of God to guide

and direct me to all that is for my highest good

and greatest expansion.

I have a wonderful present and a brilliant future.

Life is loving me and my best years are still ahead of me.

AFFIRMATIVE PRAYER TREATMENT 30

There is only ONE Power and Presence.

There is no opposition to this One Divine Source.

There is nothing to fight against nor fear.

There is no need to worry or rush about.

Spirit is the Doer and I am the channel.

I cannot predict nor control what is going to happen today.

But there is a Dynamic Something within that

responds to my thoughts, words and feelings.

I now align myself with the Infinite Presence within all.

All things in my world are accomplished

in effortless joy & cooperation.

I awaken the Creativity and Genius within me now.

I TRUST the Source to line everything up

without my manipulation.

I have no idea what should happen today for

I am on a need-to-know basis as a happy miracle worker.

I sense the Energies in each situation and

I do not force nor resist.

I am not seeking or searching.

I am invoking Higher Energies.

I RELAX into the flow of the Great Mother Tao and allow

all things to work together in harmony as I show up,

on time, prepared, doing what I said I would do,

with love, peace and Joy.

I am instructed by Source from within and expect

a day of joyous miracles and of Light.

There is nothing to fix – only an opportunity to heal.

For this I am so grateful as I now I release my day to God.

All is well, all is well, all is well.

AFFIRMATIVE PRAYER TREATMENT 31

I do not have to make anything work today.

I do not have to make anything happen.

I do not need to prevent anything.

There is nothing I need to seek or earn.

There is a Power in being present and in

relaxing all my defenses and aggression.

I do not wish to fight or rage against the tides of change.

Instead, I choose to be happy and free in my now.

I can be a positive influence today by standing

in my own Center of Truth, Peace and Joy.

In this State, I always have whatever I need.

In this defenselessness, my safety, peace and success abide.

From this place will come my strength and

I will be guided with every breath I take.

AFFIRMATIVE PRAYER TREATMENT 32

I arise and walk in gentleness today.

The peace of God is mine and I activate it now.

There is no war to fight – no enemy of the Light.

I release and dissolve all attack thoughts, all strategies,

all schemes and resentments and judgments.

I appreciate what is and I am not striving to get anything,

nor to arrive somewhere different.

I walk in tenderness today and I see a world of

beauty and Light as I am healed in gentle laughter.

All that I do is done with loving non-attachment

as I surrender it all to the Divine Presence within me.

This is a day that unfolds in effortless joyful ease

as I focus on gratitude, praise and appreciation.

There is nothing to fix, or fear, or push against.

All is well in my world.

Affirmative Prayer Treatment 33

I breathe in deeply and I am relaxed and at peace.

Nothing wavers me from my truth today as

I stand firmly in the Love and Grace of God.

Nothing disturbs me today and it is impossible

for me to contain the Love that is flowing through me now.

Life rises up to greet me as I walk through the open doors

summoning my good to me through my JOYFUL vibration.

I do not struggle, push against, argue with

or try to make anything happen.

Life is for me and none are against me as I walk in

gentleness and love today.

AFFIRMATIVE PRAYER TREATMENT 34

I walk in perfect Grace today as

I release all tendency to struggle and strive.

I show up, on time, prepared, doing what I said I would do,

with a good attitude, and I walk through

the open doors to my good.

There is no need for me to worry or rush for

I cannot fail to be at the right place at the right time as

I relax into the Divine Plan for this beautiful new day.

In my world, all is well and Life loves me!

AFFIRMATIVE PRAYER TREATMENT 35

ss my body and I bathe it in Light with

my loving thoughts and feelings today.

This body is an expression of Consciousness and there

is nothing unspiritual or unholy about it in any way.

It is a form of expression and communication whether

it is in savoring food, sexual expression, loving words and

actions or simply resting in the warm afternoon sunlight.

I bless this body just as it is and just as it is not.

It is an extension of my own Creative Imagination and

is my oldest and dearest companion –

I give thanks for this precious friend.

Affirmative Prayer Treatment 36

Success, health, money, joy, opportunities,
love and romance stalk me.
It's so easy for me to make great money
and to live abundantly.
I am wealthy and prosperous –
big money sticks to me like static cling.
Fabulous doors of good keep opening for me.
Age is just a number – I am ageless and self-renewing.
I grow more vital and attractive every year.
My best most productive years are still ahead of me.

I am doing fantastic work and business is booming!
I am inspired and inspiring.
I am peaceful, happy, loved and lovable.
I am kind, forgiving, generous and open-hearted.
My mind is clear and I have a wonderful memory
for good times.
I am quick on my feet mentally and physically.
Great things just fall in my lap all the time.
These are the good old days.

<u>AFFIRMATIVE PRAYER TREATMENT 37</u>

In my world, there is magic even in the mundane.

I am not looking for special people or special moments.

This moment is enough and I am sufficient for the moment.

By Grace, I see my world with loving gentle eyes and

I allow myself to be just as I am, and just as I am not.

Therefore, I release all others to be just as they are.

I will not push or bully myself today but instead

I walk with the Mighty Ones Who guide me

down the gentle paths of freedom, love and peace.

AFFIRMATIVE PRAYER TREATMENT 38

I trust the path I am on and I trust the process of Life.

If I find I am going in the wrong direction,

I can always turn around and get back

on the highlighted route.

The how and when of things is none of my business.

I release all attachments to specific outcomes and

if one dreams dies, I simply dream a new dream.

I keep track of my Joy instead tracking losses and gains.

When the tide goes out, no one calls this a loss or a failure,

therefore I will not judge my own life

by appearances either.

My only success is in terms of how much

peace and Joy I am allowing.

I now relax and allow myself to enjoy the journey

as I savor today's gifts.

Affirmative Prayer Treatment 39

I can always soothe my way to a better feeling place.

It's not my job to force anything for I can work with

whatever Energies are present at the moment

to make gentle progress.

One thought at a time I am able to change my vibration

to a more spacious life giving one as I shift my attitude.

I stay in my own yard and keep my eyes on my own paper

as I focus on all the positive aspects of

whatever or whoever crosses my mind.

I am making good choices today that lead

to my greater peace and Joy.

I am noticing all the good that fills and

surrounds my world today.

Whatever needs to get done today will be done by

Divine Grace within me as I take my

gentle journey up the emotional scale.

I am allowing my good to find me today.

I have called off the search and am instead lining up with

my dreams, visions and intentions for

a life of joyous abundance.

As I focus on following my JOY, the blessings that are mine

come running to me like happy puppies

rolling in ecstasy at my feet.

I open myself to all the joyous good that the Universe has

for me today and my Joy increases the Joy of all the children

of God who are open to receive it –

We are healed together in Divine Grace.

I am so happy to see what delightful surprises await me as

I walk in Love and peace and Joy.

AFFIRMATIVE PRAYER TREATMENT 40

Just as light dissolves darkness at the speed of light,
an old energy pattern can be quickly reversed
as miracles dissolve all limits and problems.

I need no breakthroughs today for I simply
turn up my Light and all fear dissolves.
Therefore, I allow my JOY to rise as I align
myself with the Power & Presence of Divine Grace.
My life unfolds in perfect ease, peace and happiness today
as I focus on all the beauty and blessings of my world.

There is no need to fix or save anyone else.
The Divine Presence within me activates that
same Divine Presence in all those who choose it.
Life is good in this bountiful magical Universe of ours.

Affirmative Prayer Treatment 41

With joyful anticipation I greet this new day
of miracles, light and glorious good.
Spirit uses my hands, my feet and my voice this day
and I am blessed in the process of being used to heal.
We are all healed together as I release everyone
into the loving care of God's ministering Angels.

I am playing in the Light today and
I expect and am prepared for divine love
and for happy opportunities to surprise & delight me.
I am gathering up the evidence that
I am connected to Source.
Life loves me and love pursues me as
I float down the Stream of Golden Light to
my greatest good and joy so far.

AFFIRMATIVE PRAYER TREATMENT 42

In my world, magic and miracles are daily happenings.

I find beauty in the most mundane and simple things

because I see with spiritual vision,

not merely by physical sight.

All around me, the fairies of the Universe conspire to Light

my path and lead me to the open doors to my greatest joy.

I expect Life to go well today for

my world is formed by my thoughts.

My world is a place of rainbows, unicorns and butterscotch

fields even while on the concrete roads

and behind corporate doors.

The magic is in me, not in the world

because that is where God placed it.

I am happy in my present and looking forward to all the

wonders that lay before me today as

I walk through the magical open doors.

I am calm, alert and ready to ACCEPT the gifts of God today.

AFFIRMATIVE PRAYER TREATMENT 43

Love and Joy are the guiding forces of my life.

I need do nothing to force anything happen for the

Divine Plan of my life operates

through attraction, not promotion.

I follow the Call to Joy instead of the drive of ambition.

My vibration is clear, strong and alive

with prospering power.

I listen to the Guidance of the still small Voice and

I know that God is on the Field.

Today I am walking through the open doors as

I recognize that right where I am, God is, and all is well.

AFFIRMATIVE PRAYER TREATMENT 44

It's a new day of new Life and new possibilities for good.

I am ready to happily swim, float and

play in the ocean of miracles.

There is nothing limiting me but my own thought

and now all old limiting beliefs are washed away in the

shimmering blue waves.

I am not afraid to be happy today.

I am not afraid of love.

I'm here to experience all the good that Life has

to offer me today as I OPEN TO RECEIVE It's gifts.

I am swimming with life today and Life is very very good.

AFFIRMATIVE PRAYER TREATMENT 45

Right here, right now, no matter what happens in my world,

all things are held perfectly in the hands of God.

From the smallest to the greatest,

everything is illuminated with the Presence.

I will not study or obsess about problems and wounds today

but will instead remember that there is no opposite to God.

There are not two powers in the Universe, but only One,

and in this One, I live and move and have my being.

There is nothing to fear.

<u>Affirmative Prayer Treatment 46</u>

I am in the right place at the right time today.

And I always have what I need.

Life loves me and things go well for me.

I am treated with favor everywhere I go

and I live by Grace rather than by struggle.

I need not chase after anything or anyone for

I am a magnet for the best that Life has to offer.

I am sailing along across an ocean of love and possibilities.

I am a grateful Child of God today & all is well with me.

<u>Affirmative Prayer Treatment 47</u>

Love and peace and joy are stalking me today.

God is obsessed with me and miracles are lighting my world

as the Universe rises up to remove all obstacles.

This is a day of endless Grace, with Angels on every corner.

I receive the gifts of God today as I share the good

with all who cross my holy path today.

I am loved and loving, happy and whole.

There is nothing to fear.

AFFIRMATIVE PRAYER TREATMENT 48

I live within a Possibility Matrix of limitless potential.

Within the Matrix, miracle follows miracle and

the flow of Creative Ideas and opportunities is endless.

There is a Dynamic Something that responds to my

thoughts, feelings and actions in this cooperative Universe.

I choose today to guide myself to the thoughts, feelings &

actions which bring more Life, more JOY,

more peace and plenty.

This is a day of alignment with the Divine Power and

Presence as I walk happily through the open doors.

I allow myself to be happy today – there is nothing to fear.

AFFIRMATIVE PRAYER TREATMENT 49

There is no competition, criticism nor

condemnation in me nor towards me.

There is more than enough good for all of us to thrive.

Everyone wins in my space, including me.

I walk and live in an atmosphere of joyful success

and all around me Life reflects my Consciousness

as my days unfold in effortlessly happy ways.

I am prepared to be delighted by Life today.

<u>AFFIRMATIVE PRAYER TREATMENT 50</u>

The Light extends not only on Summer Solstice,

but through all of my life as

my greater good keeps unfolding.

I am open to receive the unlimited blessings of

Consciousness today as I joyfully take my

emotional journey from good, to better, to best.

I focus my attention on ONLY the good today as

I give praise and gratitude to all

I see, hear, feel & experience.

I EXPECT miracles today because my summer garden

is overflowing with the beauty and order of God.

My vibration is high, holy and joyfully Helpful!

Affirmative Prayer Treatment 51

I have put love at the very center of my life.

Love is the why of everything I do and it carries me

through to completion when things get tough.

Love is what compels and impels my life and

this Love is very essence of Who and what I am.

Love lights my way today as I focus my attention on

the loves of my life – those people and things that

bring the most joy to me – music, art, friends, pets,

sunshine, children's laughter, wild flowers –

I am guided, driven, compelled and lifted up by love today.

AFFIRMATIVE PRAYER TREATMENT 52

With God ALL things are possible.

I am filled and surrounded by love and support today and

I will not let the ego steal my joy from me.

No matter what, I can always massage my own thoughts

to a better feeling place and guide

my mind to greater relief.

I do not look to others to please me or soothe me because

I am the only thinker in my own mind.

I can move my mind up the emotional scale

to a place of greater joy, freedom and peace.

As I activate this Divine Power,

miracle follows miracle in my world.

With God, ALL things are possible FOR ME!

AFFIRMATIVE PRAYER TREATMENT 53

Love is possible!

God created me as Love and as Love I remain.

There is no need to seek for what I already am.

I let go of all defenses that I used to guard my heart

so that I may experience the fullness of Grace now.

I am open, intimate, vulnerable and available for Love

in all it's many forms. I am loving, loved and lovable.

Love is not only possible – it is the only thing that's real.

AFFIRMATIVE PRAYER TREATMENT 54

There is a Divine Love alive in me today.

Everywhere I look my gaze falls on something to appreciate

as I activate the vibrations of love and gratitude in my heart.

I am Spirit infused, Guided, protected and directed.

There is nothing that I face or do alone today.

God goes with me wherever I go and

the beauty of life is more vibrant and alive

as together we bless the world with love today.

My heart and hands are open to freely give and receive.

I allow myself to be happy today.

I allow myself to feel love as

I forgive and release, relax and breathe.

AFFIRMATIVE PRAYER TREATMENT 55

I am a Mystic and a Miracle Tracker.

Like a detective I gather up the evidence and clues as

I record and build my case to prove that

Grace is loosed upon the Earth.

I am filled with wonder as I walk my path today.

Wonderful experiences just fall in my lap and

I am guided by the Light to the best opportunities.

And this is all because I have chosen to think NEW

thoughts and BELIEVE in possibilities instead of limitations.

None of it comes from the outside,

for the only Power is the Christ within.

Nothing and no one can save me – I am safe because

I choose to think safe and loving thoughts.

I look around me today and see beauty,

order and goodness.

I am co-creating my Life today with every thought I think.

The world I see is the one

I invoke through my Consciousness.

Today I am invoking the world of wonder and delight and

I fully expect miracle after miracle to light my way.

Affirmative Prayer Treatment 56

I will do my very best today, whatever that is.

My best may be a tiny fraction of what it was 10 years ago,

it may be twice what it was yesterday –

none of that matters.

In this day, this moment, I shall do my calm joyful best.

There is nothing and no one to compare myself to.

This is the only moment I can live, the only one I can be.

And I make the most of my present by BEing present,

just as I am, just as I am not.

My best changes all the time –

therefore I show up and do the best of

whatever best I have to give today.

My success has nothing to do with what is accomplished on

a "to do" list – and perhaps today's best will be a long walk

and two naps in the sunshine.

Being one's self is not stressful.

Trying to compete even with my old self is the stress that

destroys present happiness and peace.

Today, I am the best ME that I can possibly be –

whatever that means.

Affirmative Prayer Treatment 57

Today I release all tension and resistance

as I surrender into the flow of Divine Grace.

I forgive and am forgiven.

I release and am released

as I activate the Christ Consciousness within me.

Whatever I need is given me this day.

I have all that I need to handle whatever occurs today

and there is no hurry, no need to rush.

I am in perfect Divine Timing.

I keep myself in the now, focused on

the step in front of me as I breathe,

trust, love and stay in my own business.

This is a day of blessed Grace, peace and ease

and everything is unfolding for my greatest good.

<u>Affirmative Prayer Treatment 58</u>

Reality is plastic and my thoughts are creative.

Today's "facts" are just the result of yesterday's thinking.

And I can think NEW THOUGHTS today that will

create new facts in my tomorrows if

I am willing to change my mind.

Nothing ever stops or hinders me except me.

No one else is creating in my life. I am the one.

I get to choose what I BELIEVE and

what story I will tell myself.

Through my thoughts, words, attitudes and actions,

I joyfully create the life I love to live.

AFFIRMATIVE PRAYER TREATMENT 59

My mind is my good friend and servant.

It awaits my direction on what to think about and focus on.

I rule my mind, which I alone must rule.

I choose to rule with love, joy, peace and kindness today.

I focus on the thoughts and aspects of life

that stimulate JOY in me.

I am not waiting for life or other people

or God to make me happy.

I love that I get to choose how good I want to feel by

focusing my mind on the POSITIVE ASPECTS of

whatever and whoever is in my world today.

My heart is open, my mind is clear, my spirit is renewed

and everything I need comes to me today

in ease, joy and Grace!

AFFIRMATIVE PRAYER TREATMENT 60

I am blessed by the Thoughts of God today.

Wherever I go, Angels light the way with messages of

Love, peace, power, healing and beauty.

I am surrendering to the Divine Plan for my

happiness and greater good as I walk in Love today.

I remember that I am safe, that all is well, and that

all things are held perfectly in the hands of God.

As I breathe this in, my body and mind relax

and I cannot help but smile as I melt into Divine Love.

AFFIRMATIVE PRAYER TREATMENT 61

Success, joy, peace and Life cling to me

like static electricity.

I cannot shake it off no matter what I do today.

Life loves me and love pursues me.

AFFIRMATIVE PRAYER TREATMENT 62

There is a Dynamic Something in the Universe which
responds to my thoughts, words and attitudes.
This Something is Infinitely Intelligent
and is everywhere present.
I choose to Consciously use and cooperate with It now
as I choose the thoughts, words and attitudes that I WANT
increased in me and in my world.
I am a Conscious and deliberate Being of Light.

The Life that I am seeking, is now seeking me and
I welcome it with ease and calm delight.
I do not struggle or strive – I invoke, accept and allow

AFFIRMATIVE PRAYER TREATMENT 63

Good day Springtime of my Spirit!

Thank You for this beautiful day – this fresh new

opportunity to LIVE!

I am renewed in the Grace and Glory of God today

as I release and forgive the past

and stand ready for the new.

In this Grace all my needs are supplied – the love, peace,

joy, companionship, health, harmony, work, money,

homes or whatever other need arises is

met by this bountiful Source within.

I relax now and LISTEN for the Words of Guidance as

I give thanks for all that has been given,

and all that I am and God is.

<u>Affirmative Prayer Treatment 64</u>

I seek and receive the Guidance of Spirit for this day.

I am guided, led, directed, loved and cared for in all things.

The doors and windows to my good open before me and

I am joyfully used by God to Help and to Heal, all

while enjoying the day in expected and unexpected ways.

There is nothing to fear, no need to worry.

AFFIRMATIVE PRAYER TREATMENT 65

The thoughts I think and the words I speak

are creating my world for me today and for tomorrow.

I choose to create the best by expecting only good to come.

I love and honor myself because I am a child of God,

therefore I deserve and accept only that which reflects

my Divine Inheritance and I am OPEN TO RECEIVE it now.

AFFIRMATIVE PRAYER TREATMENT 66

I am sowing the seeds I want to harvest in my life.

If there is any lack in my world, I can begin to sow seeds

in that area which will reap an

abundant harvest in due season.

Today I am sowing the seeds of the harvest I want to reap.

AFFIRMATIVE PRAYER TREATMENT 67

Life loves me and is seeking me out to bless today.

I open my heart, my mind and my hands today to receive

the blessings of God as I allow Grace to

guide me through the open doors.

I gently share my blessings all those who are open to

receive me and the gifts I have to give

through the Presence within me.

Life loves me and love pursues me.

<u>Affirmative Prayer Treatment 68</u>

I have two worlds to choose from each moment.

I can choose the nightmare or the happy dream.

In my happy dream I walk about the world giving

my attention to all that vibrates with the love frequency.

Everywhere I go, I see evidence of the goodness, kindness

and generosity of people – the whole world is my

community, my family.

I am falling in love with humanity and

my heart is melting with joy.

Love rises up to greet me today as

I walk the streets of the happy dream.

A<small>FFIRMATIVE</small> P<small>RAYER</small> T<small>REATMENT</small> 69

As I devote myself to Love, I let go of "special" love

in order to have a heart overflowing with

holy love for all Life and Self.

I open the portals of my soul today to let the love blow

through like the warm cleansing winds that deliver the

pollen to make flowers grow.

My love is big, bountiful, nourishing and magnetic.

Everywhere I look today I see more to praise and appreciate

because today all fear and grievances have dissolved and

I am left with a heart full of love for all of Life!

AFFIRMATIVE PRAYER TREATMENT 70

Love is my guide to miracles today.

I will not let fear dictate my thinking or my actions.

I am learning to master my own Consciousness and

I am choosing to let love of Life, of self, of others, of God,

be the driving force behind all that I do today.

I am not merely thinking thoughts of love,

I am speaking words of encouragement, support,

soothing and acknowledgement to all those

I come in contact with, including myself.

Love is my Guiding Light today.

<u>Affirmative Prayer Treatment 71</u>

There is no criticism, competition nor condemnation

in me nor towards me.

Everyone wins in my space, including me!

Divine Love is drawing to me now all that is needed

to make me happy and make my life complete.

This a miraculous joyous day and I cannot wait

to see how Spirit handles every little detail perfectly!

AFFIRMATIVE PRAYER TREATMENT 72

I am speaking and believing in my greater good.

I will not be complicit in the ego's plan to

steal my joy and peace.

I deny that there is any power opposite to God.

Nothing that is mine by Divine Right can be taken from me.

I will not use my words to curse and deplete today for the

power of life and death is in the tongue –

my words have POWER in them.

I am speaking today of all the good

that is here and on the way.

AFFIRMATIVE PRAYER TREATMENT 73

I will ONLY speak words of blessing and increase on this day.

God is THE author of restoration and expansion.

I know that I am Who God says I am and

I can do what God says I can do.

I am not weak, but strong.

I am not diminished, but expanding.

I am not limited, but empowered from within.

The BEST IS YET TO COME IN MY LIFE!

This is not the end, but the beginning of the

overflow years in which the good is more than

enough to share and to spare.

God is faithful and I am living under God's promises.

I call today good and I look forward to the many

blessings and miracles which I will have to report

at the end of this glorious day.

AFFIRMATIVE PRAYER TREATMENT 74

I am putting first things first in my life now as

I take time today to reflect on my priorities.

I know it is not enough to say that certain things are

important to me –

I must demonstrate it through my

consistent actions and showing up.

I do not merely vision the week ahead today, but rather

actually schedule my week, making specific times for doing

the things I say are most important to me.

I am showing up, prepared, on time,

doing what I said I would do, with a good attitude.

If I say family is most important to me,

I schedule specific times with them.

If I say my health matters,

I schedule time to take care of my health.

My actions and my words are matching up these days and

it is creating a life of joy, peace and deep satisfaction.

<u>Affirmative Prayer Treatment 75</u>

Today I stand in the calm center of the Divine Presence.

Here I am Guided to all the right thoughts,

actions and attitudes.

I have given up struggle, pushing and straining as

I allow God's Joy to bubble up from within my spirit.

Everything in my life is an expression of that Joy.

I let go of separation, fear and the desire

to control people and conditions.

I expect and accept miracles today as I turn my eyes to God.

This is a day of blessings and of Light.

AFFIRMATIVE PRAYER TREATMENT 76

I surrender to the Grace and Peace of God today as

I practice gentle kindness with myself

in all my thoughts and actions.

As I am kind and loving with myself,

I am kind and loving with others.

I walk in God's Love today and I know that

I always have what I need.

This is a day of effortless Grace as I let go of MY agenda

and accept His plan in place of my own.

No matter what happens today,

I know that I am held in Light and all is well.

AFFIRMATIVE PRAYER TREATMENT 77

My body is my dearest oldest friend.

Today I deliberately move my body with joy.

I know that bodies want to move and to feel the Qi moving

through with ease. Bodies crave balance.

Today I accept and bless my body just as it is, and

just as it is not. I meet it where it is.

I do not punish, abuse, pound or resent my body.

I lovingly speak and think of every single part of it and I

speak TO IT with loving words. I pay attention to it and have

no fear, guilt or shame about it.

I move my body with love today and respect it as a dear

close friend who serves me as best it can each day. I do the

best I can with where we are today because I make the best

of things, not the worst.

Every breath I take renews the cells, the blood, the tissues

and the organs. The Life Force knows what to do to restore

harmony and perfect balance of vitality.

I am a patient, kind and loving steward

of this wonderful vehicle of Life.

I love and appreciate my beautiful body.

AFFIRMATIVE PRAYER TREATMENT 78

All my relationships are Holy Encounters in which
we meet to give and receive the blessings of God.
Today I rendezvous with wonderful people and
we bless each other with the peace of God.
I do not judge according to appearances.
I shine the Light on all those I see today.

Affirmative Prayer Treatment 79

Good morning Lord! It is another day of miracles and light.

I open my heart to receive the gifts of God and

to share my light with the world around me.

There is nothing for me to fear because I am

always guided and protected by Divine Consciousness.

This is a day of unexpected good and blessings.

My joy is rising and my peace is sustained by Source.

AFFIRMATIVE PRAYER TREATMENT 80

Every appearance of limitation is now yielding to Spiritual

Truth in the same way that darkness yields to Light.

There is nothing for me to fight against or for.

The Spiritual Truth is health, harmony, love, kindness,

prosperity, right relationships and work, creativity,

limitless expansion, wisdom, guidance and more.

I rest in the Spiritual Truth today as I am led by God

to my greatest good so far.

AFFIRMATIVE PRAYER TREATMENT 81

God loves me totally, right now, just as I am.

There is nothing I need to do to be worthy.

This vessel of Light is very worthy indeed.

Today I am a confident Child of God, going forth

to live in joy, abundance, peace, health and love.

AFFIRMATIVE PRAYER TREATMENT 82

I am a spiritual being in a spiritual Universe.
The Universe is responding to my Consciousness
and so I have the power to focus my mind on
that which brings more joy and more life to me.
I deliberately and lovingly select the thoughts
that will bring the most good into my world today.

Affirmative Prayer Treatment 83

I deliberately select my thoughts as carefully as

I would choose a precious gem at the most

expensive jewelry store in the world.

My thoughts are more valuable than any treasure

the world can offer because they create my world.

These are the precious jewel thoughts I select today:

_____

_____

_____

_____

_____

_____

_____

<u>AFFIRMATIVE PRAYER TREATMENT 84</u>

I admit that I am powerless over miracles, grace and magic;

that my life has become completely enchanted.

I admit that awesome, amazing, miraculous things

are going to happen to me today.

I look forward to seeing how Spirit unfolds this day

in perfect joyous alignment with God's happy plan for me.

AFFIRMATIVE PRAYER TREATMENT 85

I have come to believe that a Power and Presence greater
than myself is restoring me to total joyous awareness
of my Divine Supernatural Nature and that It will
run my life with ease and effortless accomplishment
of all that is good - guiding me every step of the way.

AFFIRMATIVE PRAYER TREATMENT 86

I turn my life and this day over to the Divine Power and
Presence that makes planets revolve around the Sun in
perfect proximity and to let His Angels and Guides lead me
to ever-expanding good in every area of my life –
to follow and obey directions from this loving Source.

<u>Affirmative Prayer Treatment 87</u>

I am now conducting a fearless searching miracle inventory.

I am looking for the evidence of how I am getting it right

and how love is increasing in my life every day.

I am a Special Agent of the Spiritual Underground

seeking out the clues to the existence of miracles in my life.

This is an ongoing mission and every day I get better and

better at recognizing the hand of God in my world.

This is the most exciting time of my life so far

and I am filled with gratitude and wonder.

AFFIRMATIVE PRAYER TREATMENT 88

I am admitting to God, myself and another human being the

exact Divine Nature of my manifestations of miracles and

magic through God's Grace.

I am not bragging when I tell others about the good

I am experiencing and doing because I know

that it is Spirit moving through me.

I am glorifying God by bearing witness to my progress.

It is not I, but the Divine Presence within that is the doer.

I just get to come along and enjoy the ride!

AFFIRMATIVE PRAYER TREATMENT 89

I am entirely ready for God to joyfully use and bless me
through daily miracles and to increase the manifestations of
good in me as I go about my life here on earth.
I have humbly yet boldly asked God to remove
my limiting beliefs and any habit of playing small
or in letting resistance stop me from thriving
and enjoying my life every day.
I am a miracle worker and this is a day
of Divine Harvest in my world.

AFFIRMATIVE PRAYER TREATMENT 90

I am creating an ongoing gratitude list of all those who have

been a part of these loving miraculous enchantments of

co-creating with God-Source.

I have also made a list of where I have been helpful to

others because it feels so good to

let God joyfully use me every day.

I am a grateful giver and receiver today and

I look forward to watching miracles unfold for us.

Thank You God for the wonders

and delights coming my way.

AFFIRMATIVE PRAYER TREATMENT 91

I seek and find daily for God's Will to be done in

me and in my life because I know that God's Will

is my perfect happiness.

I surrender my self-will in order for this to happen

because I know that my good intentions are not enough.

I cannot know what is best because I cannot see all the

effects of my personal will as it ripples out.

Knowing that God's Will is a joy and peace in which

everyone wins and no one loses, I happily choose it

as what I desire most for this wonderful day.

Speak Lord, I am now quiet, open and listening to

receive Your Guidance for me today.

Affirmative Prayer Treatment 92

I share my light with whoever shows up today.

I know that my words do not teach, but that to teach

is to demonstrate. Therefore, I will do my best

to demonstrate the joy and peace that are

the gifts of God, without preaching to anyone.

I release everyone to their own path, but

if they are hungry for what I have to share,

I do so gladly as Spirit guides me.

I do not decide who, and I do not sacrifice or

burn myself out to do so.

We are all responsible for our own emotional journey.

I help where and when I can, and when it works for me.

AFFIRMATIVE PRAYER TREATMENT 93

I rest in God today.

I will not struggle or strive or try to swim upstream.

I step back and let God lead the way as

I relax and breathe, relax and breathe.

I am on a need-to-know basis with Source and

if there is something for me to do, I will be directed.

If there is something for me to stop doing,

I will be told or shown in simple obvious ways.

I trust that the Universe can handle whatever comes up.

Affirmative Prayer Treatment 94

I will not judge the Children of God today or

diagnose them in any way.

It is not my job to fix anyone, but only to see the love

in even those who I find most annoying or disturbing.

If I see a "poor person" then I am judging appearances.

If I see a "rich person" then I am also judging.

I choose today only to see Daughters and Sons of God

walking the earth as my sisters and brothers.

I bless them all and I bless myself.

AFFIRMATIVE PRAYER TREATMENT 95

I gave my life to God and so it is really none of my business.

My business is to experience and share the peace of God

and to let God use my hands, feet and voice today to

do the Divine Will as I am directed and led.

This is not a religious path of sacrifice and deprivation.

Working for God is the greatest career in the Cosmos

and is the only one that brings TRUE Prosperity

and abundance of all that is good.

We get very rich doing this kind of work because

we become spiritually rich beyond all reason.

God is the greatest employer there is!

<u>Affirmative Prayer Treatment 96</u>

Everything that I touch today is infused with Light

and is blessed by the Spirit within me.

I am fulfilling my function today as the Light of the world

by focusing on the positive aspects of myself, others, the

world, and everything I see or think of because Spirit

is purifying my thoughts and restoring me to sane clarity.

There is nothing impossible for me today as I walk with God.

AFFIRMATIVE PRAYER TREATMENT 97

I embrace this new day and the miracles it brings.

I am a radiant beam of Light which attracts friends,

love, success, good health and joy.

I am not afraid to be happy today.

I am not afraid of love.

Love and acknowledgement shine on me

from all directions today.

Fabulous people are drawn to me and

love to assist me in truly helpful ways.

Our relationships are mutually beneficial

and filled with creativity and love.

We are co-creating miracles with Source!

Affirmative Prayer Treatment 98

I live in a friendly Universe.

Though the world can be harsh and unkind,

the Universe is my loving beneficent Partner,

bringing into my experience whatever I focus on.

Today I choose to focus on what there is to praise,

honor and appreciate about myself and <u>my</u> world.

I open to receive the gifts of the Universe today

as I clear my mind and open my heart.

This is a wonderful day to be me!

<u>Affirmative Prayer Treatment</u> 99

I place my future in the hands of God.

Instead of focusing on problems, I focus on God.

There is no need for me to worry or micromanage

because I know that God is on the Field!

He's got my day, my past, my present & future

in His loving hands and I can relax my mind

knowing that everything always

works out very well for me.

I am a Child of God.

AFFIRMATIVE PRAYER TREATMENT 100

Whatever I need to know is revealed to me today.

I have all the Help I need to flow joyfully through this day.

Nothing good is denied me except by my own resistance.

Therefore I relax and allow Spirit to open all the right

doors and to bring into my experience all the right people,

places and opportunities to work happy miracles.

Wonderful things are going to happen to me today

and I am a blessing everywhere I go.

AFFIRMATIVE PRAYER TREATMENT 101

Peace. Be Still.

I have the power to activate inner peace by instructing my

mind to be still instead of giving in to stressful thoughts.

I can rule my mind gently and firmly with daily practice.

I have a wonderful mind and I choose to guide and direct it

in the direction of peace and joy by taking a positive

approach to life today.

I simply say to my mind, peace, be still.

Affirmative Prayer Treatment 102

Today I choose to come from a loving place all the time.
I know that everything is either love or a call for love and so
I choose to let go of analyzing the fear and darkness of the
ego but instead to look beyond to the Light within all.
I know that I have Spirit to guide me in this and to gently
remind me of my Divine Function as the Light of the world.
Nothing feels better than coming from love and
I choose to feel good today by using
Spiritual Vision instead of physical sight.

AFFIRMATIVE PRAYER TREATMENT 103

God is with me now. There is a Divine Plan for my life.

I believe in the power of God. I believe in miracles.

I believe in the radical action of God's love here on earth.

There is no opposite to this power.

It flows from God through me now.

God uses my hands, feet and voice today to do

the Divine Will.

What a wonderful day of miracles this is!

AFFIRMATIVE PRAYER TREATMENT 104

All good is effortlessly drawn to me today.

I cannot fail to be at the right place at the right time.

There is limitless good – more than enough for everyone.

All fear and negativity are washed clean from me now.

There is no need to worry or rush –

the Universe has perfect timing.

I align myself with my greater good today and

watch as miracles follows miracles.

AFFIRMATIVE PRAYER TREATMENT 105

My work, business and all my affairs

are run by Divine Intelligence.

I always have more than enough money to pay all my bills

and to live an abundant and prosperous lifestyle.

This is a rich season of Divine Harvest.

Big joyous sums of money and resources come to me

in a steady gentle stream to meet every need.

I am a grateful happy receiver and

my work flows with limitless creativity and fun.

AFFIRMATIVE PRAYER TREATMENT 106

I am continually coming into greater harmony and alignment with those I work with – clients, co-workers, employees, and employers alike.

There is no competition and no scarcity.

I let go and dissolve any belief in conflict as I allow Spirit to guide us to cooperative successful relationships.

We all win together and bring out the best in each other.

I am a magnet for loving successful work relationships.

AFFIRMATIVE PRAYER TREATMENT 107

I breathe life in deeply today and I am relaxed and at peace.

My mind is clear and my heart is full of love for all of life.

Nothing wavers me from my truth today.

All that I need is given me.

I have no lack of any good thing.

The Universe knows where to find me and

how best to make joyful use of me.

Great things keeps falling in my lap and

I am savoring and enjoying the process of life!

Affirmative Prayer Treatment 108

I deserve love and companionship and

I am open and receptive to love today.

The Universe brings all the right people and I together and

I gratefully welcome them into my world.

I dissolve any beliefs in separation or limitation.

There are so many wonderful people in this world and

I am continually aligning with my ideal companions.

We love and accept each other just as we are and just as we

are not – there is no need to earn love or approval.

My heart and mind are open to loving companions today.

A<small>FFIRMATIVE</small> P<small>RAYER</small> T<small>REATMENT</small> 109

I release and dissolve any fear I have about food and eating.

My body is a God-vessel and I lovingly feed it without worry,

fear or obsessing because I am Divinely Guided to make the

right choices for <u>MY</u> body without guilt or shame.

I am finding my own balance all the time and I bless

everything I eat and drink instead of cursing or fearing it.

I do not use food to reward or punish myself.

I eat with joy and peace and my body responds

with radiant health and vital energy.

All is well in my world.

AFFIRMATIVE PRAYER TREATMENT 110

My family and loved ones are surrounded by the White
Light of Divine Protection – there is nothing to fear.
The entire world is being restored to peace and sanity as we
are being led by God to forgive and release one another
from judgment and attack thoughts.
There is no need for defensiveness or to resist evil.
Since what I resist, persists – I choose to soften my heart.
There is no evil, only the illusion of separation.
Today I choose to look past these illusions to the Light
beyond – to the Spirit within.
As I focus on Light, I INVOKE Light and it is manifest.
As Light dispels darkness; love dispels fear.
Today I remember to be the Light of the world instead of
the critic and judge of it. I rest in God.

AFFIRMATIVE PRAYER TREATMENT 111

When I am disturbed by anything I remember that
I don't know what anything, including this situation, means.
But if I am willing to be shown by Spirit how to perceive and
see things differently, I can have a miracle replace my upset.

I now ask Spirit to show me the Truth beyond all upsetting
appearances so that I can be at peace again.
I *choose* peace today instead of obsessing about facts.
I have consulted the Higher Authority and once again
I rest in God.

AFFIRMATIVE PRAYER TREATMENT 112

There are no limits, only limiting thoughts and beliefs.

It is not up to me to determine how miracles happen,

only to remember that "LOTS CAN HAPPEN" if

I let go of trying to control the situation.

Only God can see all the infinite possibilities for good and

there is no need for me to instruct Infinite Intelligence in

how to work everything out. My part is to align.

There is no limit to what can manifest when I align myself

with the Infinite Power and Presence of the Universe.

Today I choose to remember that:

LOTS CAN HAPPEN!

Affirmative Prayer Treatment 113

Peace is dissolving all grievances and anger in me now.

Above all else, I want the peace of God.

I let go of being right and of arguing for limitations.

I would rather be happy, than be proven right.

I release all hostages now so that <u>I can be free</u>.

I let go of focusing on errors and wrongs now.

I am shredding my files of evidence against anyone and

everyone, including myself.

As Jesus said, *"forgive them Father, they know not what*

they do" as they were stabbing and spitting on Him,

I can also know that none of us know what we are doing

when we choose to attack and defend.

Today, I choose to only gather evidence for the good

in people, in the world, and in myself.

Affirmative Prayer Treatment 114

I was not dropped off on the planet and forgotten.

I have a Divine Companion Who never leaves my side.

I may spend a lot of time ignoring this Guidance,

but it is still being given every day, all day long.

I am tuning in and listening today for this Guidance.

I know that I am loved and cared for totally by my Source.

Today, I ask for Help and then I LISTEN to the Answers that

come so that we may perform miracles together.

AFFIRMATIVE PRAYER TREATMENT 115

I am Spirit.

I am not bound by a body or trapped in the physical.

I am limitless Spirit, moving through the physical

with ever-increasing Grace and ease.

Spirit is Who and What I am.

I am Spirit.

Affirmative Prayer Treatment 116

Good morning Lord!

What miracles shall we do together today?

I am ready and available to be joyfully used

to bring more Light through to the earth plane.

Line it all up and show me what You would have me do.

Miracle working is the most fun there is and

I am eager to get started with today's list!

I will not decide who should be helped or how.

I leave all of that to You as I am on a need-to-know basis.

I release all personal responsibility and instead am a

channel for You to operate through

even if I am not aware of it at the time.

I look forward to the joy of

working happy miracles with You today.

AFFIRMATIVE PRAYER TREATMENT 117

I surrender and dissolve all fear and worry

as again I place my future in the hands of God.

God placed within me everything I need

to experience the best that Life has to offer.

When I am afraid, I am simply leaning on my own strength

instead of remembering my Infinite Source.

I now lean on God and release all future fears.

Everything is unfolding for me in perfect Divine Order

and I look forward to reporting on how it all comes together

in delightful and wondrous ways for all concerned.

AFFIRMATIVE PRAYER TREATMENT 118

Of myself I can do nothing, but there is a Presence within
me that can do ALL things through me.
I now turn to that Presence to lead and Guide me today
so that wonderful things can be accomplished with ease.
I will not judge what occurs because
I trust the Divine Process is working everything out
in perfect timing and miraculous ways.
I get my small self out of the way now to let
my True Self come shining through.
It is another day of miracles and Light!

AFFIRMATIVE PRAYER TREATMENT 119

There is nothing incurable, nothing to be feared.

In God, nothing is so broken that it cannot be restored.

No mortal "facts" can hold back a miracle from happening.

I choose to midwife miracles today and to go beyond facts.

I will not get drawn up in the drama of the

"serial adventures of the body" – not my own or

those of other people.

Today, I am midwifing miracles.

Affirmative Prayer Treatment 120

Everything always works out very well for me

in perfect ideal timing and ways.

It may not always look like it at first, so I remember to not

judge according to temporary appearances.

Instead, I reaffirm my knowledge that behind every

appearance of limitation, is an unborn miracle waiting to

come into manifestation in my world.

I INVOKE miracles by remembering that I am not alone, and

everything always works out very well for me

because I AM a Child of God.

Today, everything is working out very well for me.

AFFIRMATIVE PRAYER TREATMENT 121

I work for God, not for money or people –

not for organizations, or prestige, or power.

Working for God is the greatest job in the Cosmos.

The perks and benefits are beyond understanding

and everything is provided to do His Will with joy.

People and companies and clients may be the avenues

through which my supply comes, but God is the Source

of all my good, and I am always royally compensated.

I work for God and everything I do is done with

High Intention to glorify the Mother-Father

Who sent me. I love working for God!

AFFIRMATIVE PRAYER TREATMENT 122

I stay in my own yard and weed my own garden.

I was not sent to police the Universe or to live

under the curse of "compare and despair."

What others are doing is not my business –

that is between them and their own Guidance.

I release all hostages today as I focus on the

glory of my own garden and what I choose to

plant and grow for myself.

I am not trying to be busy but only to be fruitful.

Affirmative Prayer Treatment 123

The only thing that's really true right in this moment is,
"person reading book." Everything else is just a story in
my head – a story I enjoy or dread.

I can change it to a better story, or I can choose
to drop any story in this moment and simply return
to the peace of God by quieting my mind altogether.

I rule my mind which I alone must rule,
but I can also ask Spirit to exchange my thoughts
for the thoughts of God so that I can return to sanity
and the peace and joy that pass all human understanding.

A<small>FFIRMATIVE</small> P<small>RAYER</small> T<small>REATMENT</small> <u>124</u>

I am a confident being today.

I am filled with the confidence that I am not alone and that

Spirit goes before me making straight my path today.

I have within me everything I need to have a day of great

love, success, joy, peace and all that is good.

I now draw from the Infinite Well within

all the confidence, courage and clarity I need to

have a day of joyous miracles and fun.

I am a confident being.

AFFIRMATIVE PRAYER TREATMENT 125

Birth is not the beginning, but only a continuation.

Death is not the end, but only a continuation.

My life is eternal and all my loved ones are eternal.

Separation and loss are only temporary appearances

in the physical, but in Reality we can never be apart.

I know that dropping the body is not death but only

the release of a temporary physical vessel.

My eternal life cannot be squelched and

I can never be apart from those I love except in a story.

All who meet, will meet again for in reality,

no one has gone anywhere.

We exist in an eternal Oneness outside of which

there is nothing else.

We are timeless beings of love and Light.

AFFIRMATIVE PRAYER TREATMENT 126

I appreciate diversity and contrast in helping me choose.
Living in this diverse world culture I see diversity – things
that I would choose for myself and things I would not.
I am not here to offer endless feedback and
opinions on what I would not want for myself.
The basis of this realm is free will
and we all get to choose for ourselves.
There is no need to protest unwanted or even to give it
thought as long as I am making my own free choices.
Today I am choosing what I want for myself while
releasing all others to do the same.
I do not need to defend against what others are doing
because God is my refuge and security.

AFFIRMATIVE PRAYER TREATMENT 127

I choose to think gentle loving thoughts today.

I will not give in to attack thoughts against myself,

others, the culture or anything I see or think of

because I know my thoughts do not leave my own mind.

I want a mind that is a wonderful place to rest in so

I am choosing to turn away from attack thoughts

and turn toward thoughts of love, peace, joy & wholeness.

My mind is a wonderful place to be today.

AFFIRMATIVE PRAYER TREATMENT 128

I will not give anything the power to steal my joy today.

Whatever happens today I know that joy is my

Divine Inheritance as a Child of God and it

cannot be taken from me unless I allow it.

If anything threatens my peace and joy today

I will not react with fear and attack,

but will respond from my Higher Self.

At any moment I can take a deep breath and say:

"Child of God, do not let this steal your joy!"

as I release the thoughts back into the nothingness.

<u>Affirmative Prayer Treatment 129</u>

If I feel trapped in some mental story I have the power

to stop the story by simply thinking or saying to myself,

"THE END."

I am not a victim of my own mind or of

any stressful story that I am weaving there.

I am the story teller and I am free to end it.

I may have to do it 100 times in one day,

but each time I will return to peace and

the remembrance that all things are held

perfectly in the hands of God.

I am the story teller and I choose to

tell stories of happily ever after today.

Affirmative Prayer Treatment 130

I am happily working at Miracles Central.

No matter where I go or what I do or who is around me

I am able to fulfill my function as a miracle worker

in part of a vast Spiritual Underground.

As a Light Worker, I am here to purify the thought

forms simply by silently blessing those around me.

Often, I need say nothing at all because it is

being accomplished through me, not by me.

And each time I bless another Daughter and Son of God,

I FEEL the benefit of that blessing for we are One.

What a great day to work at Miracles Central!

AFFIRMATIVE PRAYER TREATMENT 131

Love lights my way.

My heart is soft and open today and I am in

perfect alignment with my greater good.

I notice and match up only with that which

brings more life, joy, peace, happiness,

good will, harmony and good into my world.

I don't have to make anything happen

or work harder because alignment does the work.

I see clearly today because love lights my way.

Affirmative Prayer Treatment 132

There is nothing to fear.

I know Who walks with me today and so

there is nothing to fear, no need to worry.

I walk in trust and faith that the Divine Will

is being done in and through me today.

I am confident that the road before me

is safe and secure because of Who walks beside me.

Affirmative Prayer Treatment 133

I am always at the right place at the right time.

The Universe knows where to find me and

I am never separate or apart from my Source.

Whatever I need is right here, right now,

or quickly on the way to me.

Great things just fall into my lap because

I am always at the right place, at the right time.

Affirmative Prayer Treatment 134

I am not here to get the love or approval of others.

God made me and I am sufficient and unique as I am.

I am not broken or wounded and I don't need fixing.

I am lovable simply because I exist as a God-creation.

There is no need to audition for anyone.

Love and approval are already mine.

If I <u>need</u> to change, God will change me.

If I need to be healed, I let God heal me now.

I am not a project. I am a Child of God.

AFFIRMATIVE PRAYER TREATMENT 135

Life is my friend.

I am not at war with life or with anything.

I am a peacemaker and I make friends with life.

I accept God's peace and extend it to others.

They are free to accept it or not.

I don't take it personally.

I feel God's peace in me now as I release all hostages

and make friends with life today.

AFFIRMATIVE PRAYER TREATMENT 136

I focus on the beautiful, true and holy today.

My mind is a very holy place and so I fill it with

the most beautiful thoughts and treasures today.

I honor my Divine Mind by not treating it like

a garbage dump for the culture to fill with trash.

I select and cultivate a beautiful mind today

by focusing on whatever beauty I can find.

My mind is a beautiful place to be.

AFFIRMATIVE PRAYER TREATMENT 137

I will not judge the Children of God today.

I know that I cannot judge others and be helpful to them.

I can only help if I am willing to see the Light within

instead of focusing on their mistakes or lovelessness.

Instead of diagnosing them, I choose today to

invoke the Light within them in the silence of my heart.

I give up condemnation today and replace it with blessings.

I will not judge the Children of God today.

Affirmative Prayer Treatment 138

In my defenselessness my safety lies.

If I defend myself I am closing and hardening my heart.

As I do so, I suffer and feel separate and afraid.

If I become defenseless and open, miracles happen.

I don't want to suffer. I want miracles.

I choose miracle today by letting go of defending myself.

I know that God is my refuge and security,

so there is nothing to defend against.

I am safe. I am home.

AFFIRMATIVE PRAYER TREATMENT 139

I will not argue for my limitations today.

I am a limitless Child of God and all things are possible

when I align myself with the Divine Presence.

Rather than caving in to limiting facts and beliefs,

I consult the Higher Authority and rise up!

Miracles are happening through and for me every day

as I let go of arguing for my perceived limitations.

Affirmative Prayer Treatment 140

I will not argue for the limitations of others or the world.

If I judge the world or people around me,

I will be the one at the effect of those very judgments.

I choose now to see beyond the limiting appearances

as I call forth the Spiritual Truth beyond appearances.

I am the Light of the world and so darkness has no

power at all in my Presence.

This is the function God gave me.

It is the one God gave us all.

It is great fun to be the Light of the world.

AFFIRMATIVE PRAYER TREATMENT 141

Nothing will steal my joy today.

I am responsible for my joy and I can sustain it

or use something or someone as my excuse to

let it slip through my fingers.

I choose to hit the reset button as often as I need to

today in order to keep returning to my innate joy.

I release all blame and attack thoughts

so that nothing can steal my joy today.

AFFIRMATIVE PRAYER TREATMENT 142

I will return to stillness frequently today.

I know that love is often very quiet and communicates

mostly through actions, while fear talks its fool head off.

Therefore, I will return to the inner quietness today

in order to touch the love that God placed there.

I will listen for the still small Voice instead of to

the chattering voice of fear.

Love speaks to me all through the day and

I am tuning in to hear and respond.

Affirmative Prayer Treatment 143

I have a wonderful body,

I love more every day.

It self heals and renews,

In an effortless way.

Affirmative Prayer Treatment 144

I am taking the positive approach to life today.

It is easy to fall into the temptation of playing

"ain't it awful" with other people in conversation,

but I will not curse my future that way.

I know that every word I speak is prophesying my future

and I choose to speak words of blessing and praise

that sow seeds of success into my present and future today.

I am taking the positive approach to life today.

AFFIRMATIVE PRAYER TREATMENT 145

Since I know that my thoughts never leave my own mind,

I dissolve all fear and attack thoughts with mercy today.

<u>I am the one who suffers from my attack thoughts</u> even

if *"they started it"* or I think they deserve my attack.

I will not justify my attack thoughts because keeping them

only makes me suffer longer as I marinate in them.

I choose mercy and gentleness today for myself and

all those who I think of or see, no matter how much

it seems I am justified in becoming defensive.

I choose to let God handle "them" for me instead

of trying to police the Universe.

I now know that there is no such thing as

a "spiritual warrior."

Only a peacemaker can bring peace.

<u>Affirmative Prayer Treatment 146</u>

I am the effect of God.

God the Cause; me the effect.

I am not the victim of the world I see because

the world is not a cause in my life.

Today I remember that I am only at the effect of God.

I was created in love, and I am an effect of love.

There is nothing to fear.

Affirmative Prayer Treatment 147

What others think of me is none of my business.

I am an eternal Spiritual Being – I am not a "brand"

and I am not here to shop for friends, lovers, homes,

customers, or any of the forms of the world culture.

I do not need to get anyone's vote or approval.

I am here to express my Divine Nature and to

fulfill the glorious function God gave me.

What others think of me is none of my business.

AFFIRMATIVE PRAYER TREATMENT 148

Right here, right now, there is nothing to get, fix or change.

I am simply opening to receive the gifts of God.

I relax, slow down, and breathe in the peace of God

as I let go of all self-initiated plans and schemes.

I am open and receptive to the Voice of God within me

as I am guided where to go, what to do, what to say,

and to whom. I am happy being on a need-to-know basis.

I relax into the Divine Flow of life today.

AFFIRMATIVE PRAYER TREATMENT 149

I am not here to hustle or make shit happen.

I am here to enjoy the journey of life as

I fulfill the function God gave me.

What could be more fun that being a Light

to a world living in darkness?

The Presence that Guides me goes before me

so that I do not need to struggle or push.

Of myself I can do nothing but interfere,

but the Presence within can do all things.

I step back and let God lead the way as

I allow miracles to happen through me.

Affirmative Prayer Treatment 150

I am not this body. I am an eternal Spirit Being.

The serial adventures of this body from birth is just

a story about a fictional character I've been playing.

It is not who I really am and there is no need to attach to it.

It has a wonderful use when I let Holy Spirit use it

as a vessel for sharing the Light with others.

When I think it is "me" and identify with it, I suffer.

Therefore, I bless and love it only for it's usefulness to God.

As I do that, it takes care of itself and runs efficiently and

I do not take things personally since it is not who I am.

I can therefore enjoy this body without attachment or guilt.

The "person" I thought I was, is a fictional character.

I am a timeless, spaceless, eternal Child of God.

Affirmative Prayer Treatment 151

Today and I am learning the happy lessons of Love.

I open my heart to those who are sent to me

so that I can receive and extend the peace

and blessings of God.

I am happily learning the lessons of Love today.

<u>Affirmative Prayer Treatment 152</u>

Nothing can harm me today.

Every hand that touches me is a healing hand

and every one I see is another Child of God.

I walk safely and happily through life today

as a grateful open-hearted Child of God.

AFFIRMATIVE PRAYER TREATMENT 153

Nothing disturbs my peace and equanimity today

for I am walking in the Grace and peace of God.

Any stressful thoughts dissolve quickly in

the vibration of Divine Love that flows through

my Consciousness today.

I am strongly centered in Truth and

nothing can waver me from my center.

I rest in the peace of God today.

AFFIRMATIVE PRAYER TREATMENT 154

Only good lies before me today.

As I go about my day I know that all the right doors

are opening for me, leading me to my greater good.

I am relaxed yet alert to seeing the miracles and

endless blessings that are pouring forth today.

It is a wonderful day to walk through the open doors.

AFFIRMATIVE PRAYER TREATMENT 155

Grace is my natural state of being.

I never force my good or stress about details anymore.

I know that God has already planned for my highest good.

I am attuned to God's plan for my good today and

I know that it comes beautifully by Grace.

God's Grace is more than sufficient for me.

AFFIRMATIVE PRAYER TREATMENT 156

I need only do one thing at a time.

.. ɟet overwhelmed it is only because I am believing

my thoughts or some stressful story.

I release multi-tasking and gently focus on

just doing one thing, then the next, then the next.

I relax and breathe and know that everything

is being organized and choreographed by Source.

God is in control of time and space so I know that

miracles will help me accomplish whatever needs doing.

AFFIRMATIVE PRAYER TREATMENT 157

I am a joint-heir in Christ.

Everything that the Father-Mother has is mine as well.

There is no need to hoard nor waste manna.

I appreciate my Divine Inheritance and allow

the good to flow as my daily bread.

I am royalty in the House of the Lord

and all that I need is given me.

Affirmative Prayer Treatment 158

It's not location, location, location –

it's Consciousness, Consciousness, Consciousness.

Life is not about the right time or the right place but

rather it is about being consciously aligned with Source.

Today, I focus on my alignment first and then all

other details fall into place in perfect timing and ways.

I am consciously aligned with my Divine Source.

Affirmative Prayer Treatment 159

I am beautiful because God made me.

There is no value in degrading myself because

that only insults the One Who created me.

I give thanks to God for the chance to be the me

that was created by this Loving Divine Source.

Today I love and appreciate myself as a Divine Creation.

A<small>FFIRMATIVE</small> P<small>RAYER</small> T<small>REATMENT</small> 160

I focus on the Light in others today instead of their faults.

Since my thoughts do not leave my own mind,

I know that as I extend mercy and kindness to others in my

mind, I am at the effect of those thoughts as well.

And since there is only One Mind, my loving thoughts

can be felt by all being everywhere so that we all benefit.

I feel joy today as I focus on the Light in us all.

AFFIRMATIVE PRAYER TREATMENT 161

I release all hostages today.

I am shredding all evidence of guilt in myself and others

knowing that the Higher Court will dismiss the case anyhow.

I let go of policing the Universe or being a Karma Kop.

Since I know that jailers are also in jail,

I open the cell doors and release us all

to be freely forgiven for all our errors and lovelessness.

Today, we are restored to the Self that God created.

AFFIRMATIVE PRAYER TREATMENT 162

People come into my life for a Divine Purpose,

whether they are there for a lifetime or five minutes.

I no longer try to make them stay, or get them to leave.

Instead, I focus simply on accepting that every person

is here so that I can give and receive the blessings of God.

I do not assign to them roles that I think they should fill.

I have no idea the role anyone else should be playing.

Instead, I lovingly open my heart to let the role be

revealed in perfect timing and way by the One Who knows.

What a wonderful Divine Play we are all discovering

in each moment of every day.

I am happy and open to see how it all unfolds today!

AFFIRMATIVE PRAYER TREATMENT 163

Today I am in alignment with God's perfect Will for me.

I know that God's will is my happiness and that

my inheritance is the peace that passes all understanding.

Therefore, I relax my way into alignment with the

perfect plan for a day of limitless miracles and light.

Affirmative Prayer Treatment 164

I let go of any and all idols that I use to replace God.
I know that I suffer when I look to the world as my source.
There is nothing of the world that can satisfy me for long,
but when I know God as my Source, the things of the
world can be enjoyed without attachment or aversion.
Remembering that God is my Source, I walk through the
world today enjoying the beauty and gifts of God
without clinging to them or fearing any loss.
God is so good, so good to me.

AFFIRMATIVE PRAYER TREATMENT 165

I did not come to fix a broken world or to change anyone.

I am here on a Divine Mission to let love come through me.

It is none of my business who receives it or rejects it.

Just as a Lighthouse does not jump off the cliff to

stop a boat from crashing against the rocks,

I do not have to run around trying to save anyone.

My function as the Light of the world is to SHINE

like a Lighthouse or a city set on a hill.

As I shine, people are able to save themselves

by seeing their own Light reflecting back to them.

AFFIRMATIVE PRAYER TREATMENT 166

I have Infinite Wisdom guiding me today and always.
I do not have to ask my own limited human mind what
it wants or what to do about anything.
Of myself, I cannot see the bigger picture or all the possible
outcomes of any decision that I would think is an answer.
Instead, I am in constant contact with the Source that sees
everything, including all the ripple effects of what I choose.
I constantly consult this Higher Authority to guide my
actions and to lead my feet as I continue to walk in Love,
wisdom, peace and joy. I am guided by Light today.

AFFIRMATIVE PRAYER TREATMENT 167

I am not trusting in my own puny human strength today

but am trusting in the Infinite Strength of God in me.

God's Presence in me is my safety and security in

all things that may confront me today.

No matter what is happening in my life or in

the world today, I walk in God's protective Grace.

I trust in God's Infinite Strength knowing that there is

nothing that can threaten me as a Child of God.

Affirmative Prayer Treatment 168

I release all guilt today to the Holy Spirit.

When I feel guilty I know that I have allowed the

ego thought system to steal my joy again.

I am not guilty, though I may have made some

error along the way and acted out of fear instead of love.

Therefore, I need gentle correction, not punishment.

I ask Spirit for to now correct all my errors and for

miracles to restore everything to its right place.

Let any effects of my lovelessness be undone through Grace

and let Divine Love ripple out now to all concerned.

I let Spirit guide my hands, feet and voice if there is

anything I need to do, or not do.

Speak Lord, I am listening . . .

AFFIRMATIVE PRAYER TREATMENT 169

My goal is the peace of God.

Miracles are following miracles today.

I can easily see the Light in those around me

because Christ's Light grows brighter in my

awareness every day because of my goal.

My goal is the peace of God.

<u>Affirmative Prayer Treatment 170</u>

I am making good choices today because Spirit is

guiding my thoughts, words and actions.

There is no need for confusion or ego strategies today

for I have turned my mind over to Spirit to guide.

It is as if I am being gently led down a garden path

to the most beautiful Beings Who are all glad to see me!

My mind is able to relax into open spaciousness as

I let Spirit guide all my choices and actions today.

All is well in me and in my world.

AFFIRMATIVE PRAYER TREATMENT 171

I decide who I am today.

I tell the story of me and the world I choose to create.

My past is over and does not determine the self

I choose to be unless I want it to.

I am free to be whoever I choose in each new moment.

I love the self I am today.

Affirmative Prayer Treatment 172

What a wonderful world I am living in.

My Kingdom is not of this world but the beauty of it

is being reflected in my outer world more each day.

Amazing people and circumstances are seeking me out

and moving me more in alignment with the joyous Universe.

Today I see the beauty of my Kingdom being reflected

in all that I see, or do, or think.

AFFIRMATIVE PRAYER TREATMENT 173

Nothing is being denied me except by my own t

This is a limitless and abundant Universe

that is cooperative and friendly to me.

Each day I am writing the script of my story of

living happily ever after.

Today I choose to think limitless beautiful thoughts

and watch them manifest in my world.

AFFIRMATIVE PRAYER TREATMENT 174

My worth is not established by my accomplishments.

I am worthy because God created me that way.

I do not have to earn my space on the earth.

By Grace is am blessed, prospered and healed without

struggle, strain or working hard.

I contribute because I want to and because it is fun,

not to appease some mythical being who judges.

My God is loving, generous and endlessly good to me.

I contribute to the world out of gratitude to God,

not out of obligation or fear.

A<small>FFIRMATIVE</small> P<small>RAYER</small> T<small>REATMENT</small> 175

I silently bless everyone I see or think of today.

I am a powerful Child of God and I lovingly use

that power today to extend love and peace to humanity.

I know that when I extend blessings, I FEEL blessed too.

As I bless others, my own blessings multiply without limit.

A<small>FFIRMATIVE</small> P<small>RAYER</small> T<small>REATMENT</small> 176

Through God's Grace I release all hostages and
let all grievances in me be happily dissolved.
I shred all evidence against anyone and choose
to let the Holy Spirit heal my mind of attack thoughts.
I do not do this because I am spiritual or holy,
I do it because it gives me the endless peace of God.
And above all else, I want the peace of God today.

AFFIRMATIVE PRAYER TREATMENT 177

No one can bother or disturb me unless I have decided

to believe in separation and differences.

I now remember that we are all One in God and

that my attack thoughts only hurt me.

I choose to release us together by surrendering my

thoughts to the Holy Spirit to be gently corrected.

I choose to see the Light even in those whose behavior

bothers me the most. I see it as their cry for love.

I know we are all crying out for love and so I offer the

chalice of Mercy, instead of a crown of thorns.

Together we are set free to enjoy the day.

Affirmative Prayer Treatment 178

Under God's Guidance, I live in a state of effortless
accomplishment and ever-unfolding good.
Of course there are things for me to do and I may be
very busy doing many things, but I do not struggle or push.
I am inspired and in alignment with Source, so everything
keeps lining up in wonderful miraculous ways.
I look forward to seeing the Hand of God doing
all the heavy lifting in my life today.
I bear witness to God-in-action.

AFFIRMATIVE PRAYER TREATMENT 179

I am not overwhelmed; I am perfectly whelmed.

I remember to stop and breathe frequently

when I find myself feeling like my plate is too full

of things to do and remember and such.

I let my shoulders relax, close my eyes for

an instant and let Spirit line everything up for me.

I stay present instead of getting lost in the big picture.

I do not have to belief in the myth of perfectionism.

I am under Grace and am guided and Helped in all I do.

I breathe in the peace of God and breathe out stress.

My body is relaxing in the perfect peace of God

and everything unfolds in perfect timing and ways.

There is plenty of time and plenty of help if

I will just surrender it all to Him.

Today, I am perfectly whelmed.

AFFIRMATIVE PRAYER TREATMENT 180

I am joyfully used to by Spirit today to do God's Will.

Nothing but good lies before me today as I let Spirit

guide my actions and lead me feet on toward Light.

My path is happy and all burdens are lifted as

I remember that God is moving through me.

The way that I will know love, the way that I will feel love,

is by this limitless love moving through me,

to the world around me.

What a wonderful day of bringing more Light to the world

as I let the Will of God be done joyously through me.

AFFIRMATIVE PRAYER TREATMENT 181

I release and let go NOW.

There is no process to peace, no later.

I can be peaceful right now by letting go

of stressful ego goals and thinking.

I choose the peace of God now, not later.

I accept this peace is already within me

and I activate it by focusing on it in this moment.

I close my eyes, take a deep breath, and go within.

Ahhh, there it is. The peace of God is in me now.

Affirmative Prayer Treatment 182

I am tuning in and opening to receive God's Guidance today.

Right now there is nothing for me to do or fix or change.

I am simply opening up to receive.

There is nothing to grab hold of,

nothing to push away.

I am gently opening to receive.

Now, I will be still and listen to the Truth

as the still small Voice speaks to me of love.

I tune in and receive the word of God today.

AFFIRMATIVE PRAYER TREATMENT 183

I let go of defensiveness and resistance now so

that I may be free of suffering and pain.

I have placed my past, present and future

in the Hands of God where they belong.

This is a day of Divine Harvest in which I eat of

the spiritual fruit that I have cultivated each day.

I am living by Grace and need no defenses.

I release all meaningless goals and preoccupations

so that I may remember that God-Consciousness

is my only true goal.

I am free of suffering and pain as I place my

life in the Hands of God today.

AFFIRMATIVE PRAYER TREATMENT 184

I am filled with gratitude today as

I focus my attention on the beauty of my world.

I am not a critic or judge today because I am

opening my eyes to see how good I have it.

I focus on the positive aspects of my world

and speak words of praise and gratitude

throughout this day.

I give genuine compliments and kind words

to those I come in contact with today.

This is a day of gratitude and appreciation

and since my thoughts never leave my own mind

I know that what I give, I receive.

AFFIRMATIVE PRAYER TREATMENT 185

I am aligning with the prosperous Universe!

Christ Consciousness comes that we may have life

and have it more abundantly.

Therefore, I am accepting the good news that

I am meant to prosper and thrive.

There is nothing and no one stopping me

but a limiting belief in scarcity or struggle.

I now release all such thoughts and remember

that the Spiritual Truth is Abundant Living!

Affirmative Prayer Treatment 186

I am a wonderful person and my heart is full of love.

I know that I have a lot to offer and that I am aligning

with wonderful companions with whom I can share

loving and mutually beneficial relationships.

I release and dissolve any old patterns in relationship

that do not serve me in having joyous

loving people in my life.

I am washed clean of the past by the Purifier

who restores me now to joy, sanity and inner peace.

I am a beautiful beam of Light, drawing to me

those who are ready to love, laugh, enjoy

and share this journey through life.

My heart is open to give and receive great love today.

AFFIRMATIVE PRAYER TREATMENT 187

I am a unique creation of the One Divine Mind.

There is no one just like me, no one to compare

myself with and no competition of any kind.

I love and approve of myself today as

a perfect creation of God.

I am not broken, damaged or wounded because

I was created as a self-healing and renewing Being of Light.

I accept myself just as I am, and just as I am not.

If I need to be changed in any way,

Spirit knows how to bring it about it miraculous ways

and in perfect timing.

I accept myself as a Divine Creation of God today.

AFFIRMATIVE PRAYER TREATMENT 188

I ask for and receive the Help of God today.

I am not alone for God is with me now

and I am walking in Divine Light and Love.

Whatever I need to know is revealed to me and

everything always works out well for me as

I cast my burdens on the Christ within me.

I am anointed and I have a joyous function

and all the Help I need to fulfill it with ease.

I have asked God to heal my mind of

all fear, judgment and attack thoughts so

that I may walk in Love and Grace today.

What a wonderful day to be me!

AFFIRMATIVE PRAYER TREATMENT 189

I now dissolve and release all that is no longer

part of the Divine Plan for my life.

I now open and relax into the greater good which

IS now a part of the Divine Plan for my life.

This is a day of Divine Fulfillment as I let go

of the old and open to receive the new.

AFFIRMATIVE PRAYER TREATMENT 190

The peace of God is guiding me now.

Wonderful doors are opening for me as

I let go of any need to argue, fight or have the last word.

I prefer the peace of God to being right about my judgments

because I trust the Higher Authority to set all things right.

Love does not win because it does not compete.

Love simply abides, and it abides in me now.

Affirmative Prayer Treatment 191

I am doing a fabulous job at life because

I am under Divine Instruction every day.

There is no reason to ever compare myself with

another person or with the culture around me.

I have no category and no competition.

I am a Divine Creation, doing a wonderful job

of being the wonderful Self that God made.

I am unique and no one can take my place.

Today, I savor and enjoy my life as a

unique Creation of the One Source!

Affirmative Prayer Treatment 192

Everything keeps falling into place for me as

I align myself with the Divine Will for my happiness.

I rest in the knowledge that it's a "done deal" already

and I am being guided and led to all the right actions,

resources, people, timing and connections.

I am living by Grace, and not by struggle or effort.

I relax and let Source lead the way.

Affirmative Prayer Treatment 193

No one can steal anything from me because

all that I have belongs to God anyhow.

I trust that I am always being taken care of,

so no one can betray or take advantage of me.

There is more than enough good to go around

and anything I lose is restored and increased

by the Law of Divine Compensation.

There is nothing I own, so there is nothing to fear.

Everything belongs to Source and goes back to Source.

Earth is a glorious temp job and I am simply using

whatever is most useful for my time here.

I am safe and all is well.

Affirmative Prayer Treatment 194

I am surrounded by love and appreciation all the time

because I love and appreciate myself.

The world only mirrors my own opinions and beliefs and

since I know myself to be valuable, lovable and worthy,

that is reflected back to me everywhere I go.

I respect and value myself. I know my worth.

Love and appreciation come to me daily as

I love and appreciate myself.

<u>Affirmative Prayer Treatment 195</u>

I stay in my own yard and tend my own garden.

What others are doing has nothing to do with me.

I have no interest in gossip or comparing myself to others.

I am free and they are free – we are all choosing.

What others choose to do in their garden is their business.

I am so delighted by the seeds I am sowing and reaping

that I have no time to spy on others anymore.

My life is a wonderful garden of delights and

I am pulling out the weeds of worry and fear

as I bear the fruits of love, kindness, peace and joy.

My garden is thriving with good fruit today!

AFFIRMATIVE PRAYER TREATMENT 196

My good is seeking me out today.

I have called off the search for anyone or anything.

The Universe knows where to find me and how to

bless and enrich me in limitless ways.

I relax and make myself available for the good

that is coming to me now as I open to receive.

AFFIRMATIVE PRAYER TREATMENT 197

I am happy and carefree today because

I know Who is in charge of my life.

I am relaxed and receptive to my good as

I align with all the best of Life.

I make wonderful choices every day

and my best dreams keep coming true.

What a wonderful day to be alive

in this glorious expansive Universe of good.

AFFIRMATIVE PRAYER TREATMENT 198

I am happy in my present moment.

I am not waiting for something to happen before

I start enjoying my life and my world.

Right now I can look around and find things

to appreciate and be happy about.

There are so many blessings in my world already

and I choose to focus on what I have instead

of giving my power and attention to what is missing.

I am happy and grateful in my present moment.

AFFIRMATIVE PRAYER TREATMENT 199

My income and opportunities keep increasing.

There is so much money in this world looking

for a place to land, and I am an open landing strip!

I am continually prospering and thriving under

any and all circumstances.

There is no ceiling and no limit to my financial growth.

What others are experiencing or what is happening

in the economic culture has no effect on me because

I am connected to Limitless Source of good.

I continue to be guided to happy abundance

in all that I do because I know my Source.

AFFIRMATIVE PRAYER TREATMENT 200

I make the best of things instead of the worst.

I assume the best of others and of life and

I live in a state of constant gratitude and appreciation.

I am kind, patient and loving, and this aligns me

with those same vibrations in those around me.

Instead of fault-finding and focusing on errors,

I use my intelligence to invoke the best in others

and in myself every day.

I make the best of things today and

find that the better it gets, the better it gets!

Affirmative Prayer Treatment 201

I know that I am anointed by God and

that the word Christ means, "the anointed."

I am allowing my mind to relax into its natural

state of open limitless spaciousness as

I align myself with this Christ Consciousness.

I am relaxed and receptive to watching the

miracles unfolding before me today.

I am loved and led by Grace as

I step back and let Christ-in-me lead the way

to effortless unfolding good.

AFFIRMATIVE PRAYER TREATMENT 202

I am calm and relaxed within today

no matter how busy my body may be.

Within me is a Well of Living Waters which

sustains and nourishes my spirit and soul

no matter where I am or what I am doing.

I drink deeply from this Well and find

that I have all the energy and inspiration

I need to have a beautiful day of limitless good

and harmonious relationships.

I drink deeply from the Well of Goodness today.

AFFIRMATIVE PRAYER TREATMENT 203

Nothing good is withheld from me

and no one is stopping me from happily thriving.

I have an Invisible Supply which flows forth from

the Kingdom within me.

I do not seek in the external to get my needs met.

My supply is within me waiting to be loosed by my word.

I loose it now to manifest in my world and to bless

all those who come in contact with me or think of me.

I am the rich Child of a Loving Mother-Father God.

There is nothing good withheld from me.

AFFIRMATIVE PRAYER TREATMENT 204

Wonderful things are unfolding before me today

as I relax and open my heart to God's Grace.

I remember to breathe deeply this Grace

and to let it dissolve any worry or fear that may arise.

I expect a day perfectly choreographed by

the Infinite Artist of the Universe within me.

I am steady and sure as I walk in perfect Grace today.

Affirmative Prayer Treatment 205

I do not judge according to appearances today

because I know they are temporary manifestations.

I look beyond the physical to the Light which animates.

From this Light emanates the good, the true and the holy.

I am invoking this Light to illumine my world and to

mold the physical into wholeness, peace and joy.

I do not react to appearances,

I create content with my Higher Consciousness.

I am witnessing the Christ today as

I look beyond appearances to the Light within.

AFFIRMATIVE PRAYER TREATMENT 206

There is nothing to fear.

I know Who walks beside me today so

I walk in peace and perfect confidence.

There is nothing that my Companion cannot do

and so I do not lean on my own limited understanding

but instead lean on the Kingdom within to

guide and direct my actions, thoughts and perceptions.

My mind is lit with peace and calm today

as Christ heals my mind of all fear thoughts.

I am not afraid, because I know Who walks beside me.

AFFIRMATIVE PRAYER TREATMENT 207

God Consciousness within is creating my day today.

I step back and let this Consciousness

light the path before me as I bear witness to miracles.

I am a miracle worker because I focus my attention

on giving and receiving the peace and blessings of God

everywhere I go today.

This is my function and this is my purpose.

It gives meaning and content to all that I do today.

My part is important and essential to God's Plan.

I accept it gladly because I am a joyous miracle worker!

AFFIRMATIVE PRAYER TREATMENT 208

I do not let the culture dictate or dominate my thoughts.

I know that the world culture is rooted in fear, attack

and scarcity thinking, and this is not what I want.

Instead, I choose to listen ONLY to the Voice within me

that reminds me of the beauty and kindness of Life.

Cursing and fearing the darkness is useless, so

I choose to turn up my Light no matter the circumstances.

I am the Light of the world and I treat my mind as a

holy vessel and not as a dumping ground for the media.

I choose to fill my mind with love, peace and Light today.

AFFIRMATIVE PRAYER TREATMENT 209

Wonderful people are drawn to me and we

bring out the very best in each other.

I praise and compliment the people around me

and watch them blossom like flowers in the sun.

We encourage and uplift instead of tearing down.

The more we praise each other, the more there is to praise.

In work and play, I attract and bring out the best in others

and this blesses and enriches my world in amazing ways.

I love people, and people love me!

Affirmative Prayer Treatment 210

I thrive under any and all circumstances.

I am not a victim of the world I see or of

any current circumstances in my life.

There is a Divine power and Presence within me and

so I know that I am under no laws but God's.

God's Truth is abundance, health, love, wholeness,

peace, right work, happy companionship,

limitless opportunities & resources, creativity and genius,

loving support and life without end.

I choose to see myself as a thriver, not a survivor.

I choose to see myself as a beloved Child of God.

Affirmative Prayer Treatment 211

I am no longer curious about disturbing news.

I am most curious and interested in that which

inspires, uplifts, soothes and guides me to

greater joy, peace, happiness and love.

I give my full attention to praising the good

and amplifying all the blessings in my world.

AFFIRMATIVE PRAYER TREATMENT 212

There has never been a better time to perform miracles

than now, today, this moment.

There is nothing I need to wait for because the Universe

is ready every moment of every day.

Opportunity only knocks once; once every moment.

There it is again, there it is again, there it is again.

This is the perfect time for me to have a day

overflowing with joyous loving miracles.

AFFIRMATIVE PRAYER TREATMENT 213

The Law of Increase proves that what I praise
grows and expands in my world and consciousness.
Today I am verbally praising all the good that I see.
I am handing out sincere compliments in abundance
and watching the joy it spreads across my Kingdom.
The more I praise, the more there is to praise.
The more I give thanks, the more there is
for me to be grateful for!
Today I am pouring out praise and watching
how my own cup keeps filling itself back up
and running over with great good.

Affirmative Prayer Treatment 214

I am making a positive difference in the world

through the love and kindness I am sharing.

I am a loving and generous spirit and I am guided

by God where to give my gifts and when.

I do not give out of sacrifice, but out of the

abundance of the Kingdom within me.

I am giving love and kindness because

I know that I am an abundant being.

I give out of the great treasure of my heart

and it comes back 1,000 fold and more.

<u>AFFIRMATIVE PRAYER TREATMENT 215</u>

I am free to live the life I choose.

I am not in bondage to any person, place or thing.

As a Child of God I have Infinite Resources and wisdom

to create a life that I love living!

I boldly and consistently keep moving in the direction

of my greater good by aligning with it, not forcing it.

I take the actions Spirit guides me to take and

I know I am moving steadily in the right direction.

I am free to live the life I choose.

Affirmative Prayer Treatment 216

I dissolve and release all past grievances and resentments.

I do not have to go over them individually or even

remember what they are or were.

I give them to Spirit to shred and dissolve as

I now release all hostages and release myself.

I let go of the past and accept that I am now healed.

I am not looking in the rear view mirror of life –

I am looking at the beautiful road ahead of me

and looking forward to all I will experience and see.

The past is over. It can touch me not.

AFFIRMATIVE PRAYER TREATMENT 217

My relationships grow more wonderful every day.

I let go of trying to change or fix others –

and of trying to change or fix myself.

I am practicing loving acceptance of us

just as we are, and just as we are not.

I release any hardness of heart that I may have

developed over the years and I now

declare that it is safe for me to love deeply and fully.

My relationships are not ego attachments to bodies,

but are spiritual assignments in learning to

give and receive the peace and blessings of God.

My relationships grow more wonderful every day.

Affirmative Prayer Treatment 218

Since time is an illusion, there is no need to rush.

Everything in my world is happening in

the perfect time-space sequence for me and

for the highest good of all concerned.

I merely show up, prepared, on time,

doing what I said I would do, with a good attitude.

All the rest is out of my control.

I let go of the illusion and stress of control as

I accept the Grace and peace of God.

This is a day of gentle happy miracles.

AFFIRMATIVE PRAYER TREATMENT 219

I feel lighter and more buoyant every day.

Any heaviness of the past keeps falling away

and my spirit, heart and mind rise up, up, up.

My joy is like a cork bobbing on the surface of

the ocean, floating along without resistance

but merely enjoying the waves and movement.

I allow myself to grow more light-hearted

with each passing day.

Affirmative Prayer Treatment 220

I am not a victim of anyone or anything.

Whatever has happened in my life,

I am still here and today is another new day for me.

I will not cling to old wounds nor try to suppress them.

I surrender them to the Holy Spirit to heal as

naturally as a cut heals on my hand if I don't pick at it.

I do not make healing happen; it's a natural process.

I will not interfere with my healing by picking at old wounds.

I do not hide my scars nor glorify them –

they are the evidence of the miracle of natural healing

and so I see them as proof that I am always okay.

There is nothing that Spirit cannot heal if I will

simply allow the process to happen without interference.

I heal naturally and in perfect timing.

There is no rush. I trust the process of Life.

AFFIRMATIVE PRAYER TREATMENT 221

I notice the abundance of the Universe around me.

There is so much good flowing forth every day –

so many flowers, trees, birds, stars, grains of sand!

This must be an abundant world of plenty

and I am an important part of it.

Therefore, I am being supplied as I open up

to let Source flow through me.

There is so much money floating through the air

and I open to let it flow to me now.

There are limitless opportunities flowing forth

and I open to see and receive them now.

My world is abundant and I am limitless.

AFFIRMATIVE PRAYER TREATMENT 222

I am becoming clearer all the time about what I believe.

I know that I can shift and change my beliefs whenever

I choose as I sift through my life experiences.

Whenever I notice a limiting belief I have,

I simply release it back to the nothingness

by neutralizing it with an opposing thought of

possibilities for more expansive good.

Today, I pay attention to what I believe and

choose to take a positive approach to my life.

AFFIRMATIVE PRAYER TREATMENT 223

I am surrounded and filled with Love today.

This love leaves no room for fear or judgment

in my consciousness and it dissolves all limiting beliefs.

I open my heart to this Divine Love like

a flower taking in the radiant morning sun.

I send this love back out as a beacon to

light the way today.

I am a lighthouse of Love today.

Affirmative Prayer Treatment 224

As a Child of God, nothing is impossible for me.

I am not bound by the laws of aging, genetics, time & space.

My good can come quickly at any time.

My healings and manifestations have nothing to do

with past precedent or what any expert thinks.

I am under the Grace of God and I live in the miraculous.

The field of possibilities is limitless for me as

I align myself with the Great Source of all Life.

AFFIRMATIVE PRAYER TREATMENT 225

I am happy in my now and optimistic about my future.

There is great good before me as I continue to

expand my ability to believe in miracles and Grace.

Current economics, trends, political situations and

cultural happenings have nothing to do with me

because I live by Grace and not by works of the flesh.

I expect and accept miraculous unfolding good

today as I step into the Greater Reality

of God's limitless bountiful Grace for me.

Affirmative Prayer Treatment 226

I am not a body, therefore I have no age.

I am an eternal vibrant living Being of Light

temporarily using a physical body while on the earth.

This body reflects my consciousness and

my dominant Consciousness is as a Divine Child of God.

I do not expect decline in the coming years.

I believe that the better I get, the better I get.

I am not counting the years, I am counting the miracles.

Affirmative Prayer Treatment 227

I am interested in life, love, joy, peace and kindness.

I am interested and attracted to the goodness that

life has to offer and to growing in my capacity

to give and receive the blessings of God.

Each day is a new adventure in expanding my awareness

of how wonderful Life is and in seeing how much of

God's vibrant energy I can channel into my world.

Today is a day of gently steady unfolding good

for me and all who choose to receive it.

AFFIRMATIVE PRAYER TREATMENT 228

I dwell in the Kingdom within, therefore
gentleness and mercy shall follow and precede
me all the days of my life.
I let go of any attack thoughts that may arise
about myself or any other being no matter
how much evidence and justification there may be.
I choose to extend gentleness and mercy because
that is what the Kingdom within me is built on.
I accept gentleness and mercy for my own
mistakes, and I extend it to others for theirs.
I judge us not according to appearances and evidence,
but instead extend the peace and blessings of the Christ.
What I give, I also receive. What I extend, I accept.

AFFIRMATIVE PRAYER TREATMENT 229

I am open to experience the JOY of Life today.

It feels so good to laugh and not take things so seriously.

I am learning to laugh at my own ego thoughts

and the more I do, the less I suffer.

I am laughing at my own ego thoughts and

replacing them with the thoughts of God.

I must laugh at all ideas of scarcity and sacrifice

when I remember that the Children of God

are joint-heirs in Christ and can lack nothing good!

I am under the Christ Trust Fund Program and

so I laugh at the idea that there is anything to fear.

Affirmative Prayer Treatment 230

There is only one power and Presence.

There is nothing to oppose God; nothing to battle or fight.

I need not "resist evil" because what I resist will persist.

Instead, I turn away from the darkness and toward Light.

I invoke this Light by activating It within myself.

I no longer see teams, sides, or enemies.

I am focusing on oneness and know that

in that Oneness, all is well.

If I am afraid today, it is because I am believing

in the lie of separation and opposing sides.

I claim my miracle by remembering that

there is only God, God, God –

and I am One with God, now and forevermore.

Right here, right now, even if things are not to my liking,

all things are held perfectly in the hands of God

and I am safe.

AFFIRMATIVE PRAYER TREATMENT 231

I am using my mind constructively and positively.

I don't have to believe everything I think.

I can question my stressful thoughts, turn them around

and release the stressful ones back into the nothingness.

I get to choose what I allow into my mind

and the thoughts I will entertain and make welcome.

Today, I choose the thoughts that feel good

when I think them. I take a positive approach.

I don't have to think the most affirmative positive

thoughts anyone has ever thought.

I can simply reach for a better-feeling thought.

I am taking responsibility today for guiding my

mind to the thoughts that have more breathing space.

Affirmative Prayer Treatment 232

Wonderful things are going to happen to me today.

I am opening my mind and heart to see the beauty of life.

Life is blessing us all and I am open to see it today.

I take all the good personally and let the rest go.

Every flower, tree, bird and kindness is a gift from Source.

I choose to give everyone a break today as

I overlook all rudeness, mistakes and ugliness.

I am making the best of things today instead

of getting off track by policing the world.

The more I focus on the wonderful things,

the more wonderful things keep happening for me.

AFFIRMATIVE PRAYER TREATMENT 233

I am approaching life with courage and confidence today.

I have so much to offer and I am letting the world see it!

People love me, and I love people.

I forgive and release the past and am open

to new opportunities, new people, and new life.

Everywhere I go today I am drawn to the

highest and best that Life has to offer.

I see and appreciate Life's beauty as

I move confidently in the direction of my good.

Affirmative Prayer Treatment 234

New thoughts and ideas are coming to me

and bringing with them all the resources for their

joyous fulfillment and successful manifestation.

I am a creative and talented unique individual

with God-bestowed gifts to share with the world.

I have faith and believe that I have a Divine Destiny.

The Power and Presence that created me is also

guiding and sustaining me in fulfilling my dreams.

Love and opportunities surround me and

I am being led to the right open doors

for my greatest good so far.

It's another day of miracles!

<u>Affirmative Prayer Treatment 235</u>

I am patient as I persevere and go in the direction

of my goals and greater good in life.

I do not let obstacles stop or discourage me.

I know that with Source there is always a way and

so I lean on God instead of leaning on man.

I can rest and regroup when I need to

but I can then carry on and take the next step forward.

I congratulate myself for each step forward

and allow it to inspire me to keep going.

I release the timing and my pictures of how things can

happen to Source to work out in wonderful ways

as I continue to patiently go in the right direction.

I am patient as I persevere in working miracles.

AFFIRMATIVE PRAYER TREATMENT 236

There is plenty of the good to go around.

I am not living under the illusory scarcity principles.

I am a conduit for abundant miracles of every kind.

I always have whatever I need, with plenty so spare & share.

I live under the Universal Prosperity Principles believing that

Jesus came to show us how to live life more abundantly.

I am ready to let limitless good flow through and to me

as I tap into the Infinite Source of all good today.

My age, past, location, personality – in fact, nothing at all

can limit the Abundance Principle unless I use them as

an excuse to cut myself off from my good.

I am not making excuses.

I am claiming my fabulous Divine Inheritance today.

Affirmative Prayer Treatment 237

I am enthusiastic about the possibilities of this new day.

I look forward to watching how Spirit works

out all things for my highest good

as I am joyfully used to do God's Will.

I offer my heart, hands and voice today

to be truly helpful to whoever I am guided to help.

I know that we will all be blessed as

I happily give and receive the peace of God today.

AFFIRMATIVE PRAYER TREATMENT 238

No one can take the good that belongs to me.

I am never rejected. I am merely spared.

If a door slams shut in front of me,

it is for my own greater good and

I have been spared from wasting my time or energy.

There is another door that will open for me

In the perfect ways and timing as

I keep my heart and mind open

to the Guidance of Source.

My feelings are not hurt for I believe that

the wisdom of Source is sparing me and

guiding me to a better way to go.

I am guided and gently corrected as I go.

<u>Affirmative Prayer Treatment 2</u>

I am worthy of the gifts and Guida

I am not timid or shy in asking Spirit

I know that it is God's good pleasure to give me

Kingdom and I am in alignment to receive it today.

I know that Life is responding to my Consciousness

and I have a Consciousness of receptivity today.

This is the perfect day for dreams to come true.

I do not have to wait for better conditions or appearances

in my world before I can receive my greater good.

I am worthy now, and I am opening to receive now.

It is impossible to earn the gifts of God or

they would be wages and not gifts.

I need only be an open gracious receiver

in order to accept the blessings of God.

I am an open gracious receiver today.

AFFIRMATIVE PRAYER TREATMENT 240

I encourage and cheer myself on today.

I let go of all self-criticism and attack because

I know that is an attack on a Child of God.

I extend kindness, gentleness and mercy on myself today

as I go about my daily comings and goings.

I let go of perfectionism and impatience with myself.

I take note of even my smallest successes instead of

dwelling on or amplifying my mistakes and shortcomings.

I am on my own team today, cheering myself on

as I amplify every bit of good that I can find in myself.

I am building myself up instead of tearing myself down.

I am not better or worse than others.

I am not competing with anyone.

To say I am on my own team means that I am

for activating love in myself instead of fear.

I am cheering myself on today.

Affirmative Prayer Treatment 241

I do not contract or minimize.

I think, dream and act expansively.

I am generous and giving because

my Source replenishes me constantly.

I am able to act on my guidance and to

follow through to the magnificent successful results.

I enjoy completion and I allow myself to

enjoy the entire process from start to finish.

Affirmative Prayer Treatment 242

There is always a wonderful demand for my gifts & talents.

There are people seeking me out right now so

that we may have mutually beneficial partnerships.

My mailbox, phone, computer and more are all

great avenues for my continued success and prosperity.

Source knows just where I am and how to find me

for the most wonderful connections.

I am on the radar of the ideal creative, joyous, successful

people for work, love, play and friendship.

Everything comes in perfect amounts at the perfect time.

I am neither bored nor overwhelmed because

it all flows perfectly in and out, in and out, in and out.

AFFIRMATIVE PRAYER TREATMENT 243

I am comfortable making decisions and then

taking positive action based on my decision.

The Universal GPS directs me once I have

made a decision about my destination

and I am guided and course-corrected all along the way.

I enjoy making decisions and savoring the journey

once I have decided where I want to go.

There is no rush, no stress.

I always arrive at the perfect time.

Affirmative Prayer Treatment 244

This is an abundant Universe.

There is enough good for me and for all others.

We are all capable and responsible for our own good

for we draw from a Limitless Divine Source.

Miracles are given by those who temporarily have more,

to those who temporarily have less.

No one is more connected to Source than another.

I know that all those I choose to help are no less than myself

and I do not pity them or see them as victims.

I help because it feels so good to help and

because I have been helped and will need it again.

We are all interdependent and are able to be of use

to the whole through our loving participation in life.

Source is our Source, but Source acts *through* people.

Today, I remember that all have equal access to Source,

and I allow Source to joyfully use me as an avenue

to deliver miracles to those who are open to receive.

<u>Affirmative Prayer Treatment 245</u>

I allow others to contribute to me and

I make it easy for them to do so.

I release all false pride and resistance as

I open to receive God's Help *through* other people.

I let go of victim/martyr thinking.

I let go of thinking I have to do everything myself.

If I need help, I ask people specifically for that help and

then I truly release them to say yes or no with no guilt.

I let go of thinking others can read my mind or

thinking they *should* know what I want.

I make it easy for others to contribute to me

instead of making it more difficult.

It is not weakness to ask for help.

It is intelligent and strong to ask for

and receive the loving contributions of others.

I am open and happy to receive today.

Affirmative Prayer Treatment 246

I am learning to say no to what does not serve me.

I do not have to get sick to say no or to "get out of"

doing things I do not want to do.

I do not have to make up stories or excuses

for the choices that I make in life.

I release others to do the same with me.

I now release guilt and manipulation from

all my relationships as I give us permission to

tell the truth without attack or defensiveness.

I keep my heart open and I speak from

kindness and love, but with firmness.

I am saying no when I mean no,

and yes when I mean yes.

It feels good to live from my truth.

AFFIRMATIVE PRAYER TREATMENT 247

When I set my mind to something

I know that I am able to accomplish wonderful things.

God gave each of us free will to choose how

we will perceive ourselves, our life, and the world.

I am no longer making excuses about anything.

I am not trying to fit in anywhere.

I let go of trying to please an insane culture.

I no longer go after goals that the culture has set for us

because they either fail or do not bring me peace.

I am setting my mind only on those things that

inspire and uplift me from now on.

I am setting my mind and keeping it set

on the things that I feel passionate about

and I know that when my mind is set,

miracles follow.

AFFIRMATIVE PRAYER TREATMENT 248

I am dropping the blame-game from my life

so that I can play the PRAISE GAME.

Finding fault with the world and people in it

only brings me stress, anger and frustration.

I am now turning my full attention to all the

wonderful Answers, instead of the problems.

I am giving my life energy to taking a positive approach.

The more I feed the positive Answers,

the more the negative problems fade away

from not being fed by my energy.

I am feeding the positive approach in my life

by playing the PRAISE GAME.

I take time to thank and acknowledge anyone

I see making a positive difference.

I encourage and support those who are helping

instead of cursing and blaming those I judge.

I am taking a positive approach to life.

AFFIRMATIVE PRAYER TREATMENT 249

I am amplifying the good today and finding

positive aspects to activate through my attention to them.

More and more I find my life expanding and becoming

interesting and engaging through the Law of Attention.

I am drawn to and am drawing to me wonderful

stimulating and satisfying experiences on a regular basis.

The fun factor in my life is increasing with each

passing year and day that goes by.

I am not heading toward decline in any way.

I am heading toward expansion and satisfaction

as I amplify the good that I see all around me.

People love me and I love people.

I am hitting my stride as I let Spirit guide me.

Affirmative Prayer Treatment 250

Every day in every way, I am getting better and better.

And every day in every way, my life gets better and better.

I am so blessed to know these Principles of creation

so that I can choose how to perceive myself and my world.

I let God bless me beyond all past precedent as

I continue to dissolve and release all limiting beliefs.

I let go of any resistance I may have to thriving and

enjoying my life to the fullest.

Every day in every way, I am getting better and better.

Affirmative Prayer Treatment 251

I am seeing my good more clearly today.

I know that there is no need to seek or search

because my good is already here in my life

waiting for me to recognize it.

Today, I am relaxing and letting myself

see my great good coming into focus.

A<small>FFIRMATIVE</small> P<small>RAYER</small> T<small>REATMENT</small> 252

Magical and wonderful things happen to me

every day, including today.

In my world, there is bountiful good,

enough to share and to spare.

I go forth today knowing that I am

in alignment with the best that Life has to offer.

AFFIRMATIVE PRAYER TREATMENT 253

I only tell happy stories about myself and my life now.

I have let go of the dead past and am opening

up to the limitless good that Source has for me today.

I dissolve any mental patterns of scarcity or attack

and rest in the abundance and peace of

the Kingdom within me as

I watch it manifest in form before me.

My world is a welcoming and happy place today.

Affirmative Prayer Treatment 254

I no longer argue for my perceived limitations.

I am a limitless eternal Spiritual Being and as such

I am under the Grace of God's overflowing inheritance.

I need do nothing but open to accept it now by

affirming that there is nothing limiting or stopping me.

I no longer argue for the limitations of others.

Instead, I release them and know that

Spirit has got them and they are being led and

guided in perfect timing and ways too.

I release us all to live in freedom and peace.

AFFIRMATIVE PRAYER TREATMENT 255

There is nothing more fun that the spiritual life.

Pain and suffering have no purpose except as

the contrast and remind me of what I *do* want instead.

As I know what I don't want, I know what I do want.

Any pain or suffering is only an alarm to wake me up

from the belief in separation and fear so

that I can again rest in God's loving Grace and peace.

I can spiritually grow through joy and peace

more effectively than through pain and suffering.

The spiritual life is a life of joy!

Affirmative Prayer Treatment 256

My tolerance for joy, pleasure and fun is increasing.

There is no limit to how great I can feel and

I release any guilt or inhibitions around enjoying life fully.

There is no such thing as "having too much fun."

I can accomplish many wonderful things even

while I am having fun and enjoying what needs to be done.

I let go of any religious notion that God wants me to

sacrifice or that serving the Light means manifesting

like and ascetic or moving to India unless I love India.

It is God's desire that I be happy and

I share that desire with God.

I am becoming more and more comfortable with

a life of joy, pleasure, peace and fun.

AFFIRMATIVE PRAYER TREATMENT 257

No one needs to acknowledge or understand me but me.

I am not a beggar seeking the approval or understanding

of the people or world around me. That's my job.

As I acknowledge and understand myself,

I am in alignment with those who will reflect that back.

I am not auditioning for life. I already got the part.

I get to be me! This is a wonderful role to play!

I am learning to understand and appreciate myself

and I release the belief that I need others to do it for me.

I am loving playing the part of wonderful wonderful me!

Today, I am giving myself the understanding and

acknowledgment that I desire.

I have freed the hostages again.

AFFIRMATIVE PRAYER TREATMENT 258

God is using my hands, feet and voice today to

accomplish the Divine Will with ease.

I have no idea what anyone needs or how to help them.

Instead, Spirit is arranging and choreographing all

the details for the perfect unfolding of miracles.

I realize that the miracle may be saying "no" to someone

or some other action that may seem "unspiritual" to

the ego thought system which judges by appearances.

Therefore, I will not judge according to appearances but

rather assume that God is in control here and that

everything is unfolding in according with the Divine Will.

I step back and let Him lead the way.

AFFIRMATIVE PRAYER TREATMENT 259

I relax into the state of calm delight today.

I am not attached to outcomes so

I do not despair when things seem to go wrong

nor get off center with overexcitement when

things seem to go right.

I relax in gratitude and calm delight as

I watch with wonder a day of miracles

leading me back to God, God, God.

Affirmative Prayer Treatment 260

I am free to create and live the life I choose.

What others are choosing and creating is their business.

No one else can create in my experience unless

I want to use them as an excuse for getting off track.

My mind is very powerful and it is

always creating through what I am focusing on.

I take charge of consciously creating what I want

instead of creating by default what I don't want.

Right now, I am setting my internal GPS

to guide me in the direction of what I want to see today.

There is no hurry or rush – no need for intensity.

I relax and allow my guidance to kick in

as I proceed to my joyous highlighted route

and I release all others to do the same.

I stay in my own lane, in my own business

as I create the day I choose.

AFFIRMATIVE PRAYER TREATMENT 261

My limitless good keeps emerging before me

in wonderful effortless ways now.

It is not subtle or difficult to see because

it plainly announces itself to me,

"Here I am" and I am alert to welcome it.

I love watching my blessings emerge as

I RELAX and let it come in perfect timing

and wonderful ways.

Affirmative Prayer Treatment 262

I am seeing with Spiritual Vision rather than

judging by the appearance of physical sight.

Spiritual Vision shows me the way and

lights up my path with love and abundant good.

I am lining up with the best today as

I go forth to see and receive the gifts of God.

There is nothing to search for or strive after.

My Source knows where to find me

and how to get me where I need to be.

AFFIRMATIVE PRAYER TREATMENT 263

Divine Mind limitlessly and effortlessly meets my needs

as I turn within to the Well of Infinite Supply today.

In this Divine Mind all is One and what is known in

one place is simultaneously known everywhere.

Since there is no separation in Divine Mind

I am not sending out thoughts or trying to effect anyone

or anything with my thinking.

I am simply knowing the Truth and that Truth

is then known all across time and space.

The Divine Truth is always love, Life, peace,

prosperity, health, wholeness, and limitless good.

I am knowing the Divine Truth about myself today

and letting it guide me through the right doors.

Affirmative Prayer Treatment 264

Whatever I need to know is being revealed to me today.

I am never bereft of help that knows all answers to every

issue or problem that could ever confront me.

I am in the right place at the right time today

to see and accept whatever help I may need.

Things are always working out very well for me

and I am radiating gratitude for the help I am given.

AFFIRMATIVE PRAYER TREATMENT 265

I release the need to be right or to have the last word.

It is not my job to enlighten or correct other people

or the world at large with my "good ideas."

Everyone has equal access to Source so

I let go of trying to save others or to police the Universe.

Instead, I let God guide me to those whom

He wants to help through me today.

We will find mutual benefit and blessings

as we are healed together by Spirit.

I know that it will happen without tension or fighting.

It will happen in natural wonderful ways and

I release myself from attachment to any outcome.

I place us all in the Hands of God where all is well.

AFFIRMATIVE PRAYER TREATMENT 266

I am comforted by the Holy Spirit.

I know that there are things which are simply too big

for me to handle with only my small human self.

But God-within-me can handle all things and

make all things possible regardless of how big or small.

The Divine Mother-Father within is Love Itself

and when I feel weak or afraid, I can lean

on the everlasting arms to give me strength and peace.

No matter what happens in my world,

I know that I can be comforted by the Holy Spirit

and taken safely through any storm.

AFFIRMATIVE PRAYER TREATMENT 267

Nothing can separate me from the Love & Presence of God.

No matter how many mistakes I make or how many

times I fall down and fail myself or others,

I know that God loves me and can restore me

to peace, joy, sanity and inner peace if

I will simply ask and then allow it to happen.

I choose to let God restore me now and

to guide me in my thoughts, words, actions

and perceptions so that I may be of joyful use.

Affirmative Prayer Treatment 268

When I have reacted lovelessly, defensively or attacked

anyone, I know it is because I forgot Who my Source is

and fell into fear, judgment and separation.

I am responsible for my behavior and my thoughts

and I ask now that they be corrected by Holy Spirit

and that anyone I may have harmed now be

held in Light by God's ministering Angels

as I surrender us into Divine Care.

I allow this miracle to happen through me and

I know that we are being restored to inner peace.

I accept and extend the Atonement to all concerned

as we are washed clean by the Living Waters of Grace.

And so it is. And so I let it be. Amen.

AFFIRMATIVE PRAYER TREATMENT 269

I have the gentle Spirit of a Lamb of God

and the powerful Presence of a Lion.

No power that is not of God can touch me.

No illness or dis-ease can affect me.

No scarcity can come near me.

No loss cannot be absorbed by my

Infinite Divine Inheritance.

I am renewed and restored every moment.

I am One with my Source.

I am living as a Divine Being.

I am at home in the Kingdom within.

This is a day of Divine Harvest for me.

Affirmative Prayer Treatment 270

I am making a positive difference in the world today

by the Light that I carry with me wherever I go.

I encourage, uplift, soothe, inspire and love generously.

I am a vessel of Divine Mind and I join with those

who are aligning as Light Workers today.

There is nothing more fun or prospering than

working in the Army of Light on earth at this time.

The Light in me is going forth to touch the Light in others

and we are being uplifted and encouraged as

we make a positive difference in the world today.

There is no arrogance in this, no pushiness or attachment.

I go where God sends me and enjoy the journey

because it is not me doing it, but rather the loving

Presence within setting all things right.

Affirmative Prayer Treatment 271

Knowing what I don't want only has value

in clarifying what I *do* want.

Instead of focusing on what I don't want,

I allow the contrast between wanted and unwanted

to help me focus only on what I *do* want today.

I release the past and focus on the road ahead.

I am the one who sets my destination by

what I choose to focus on and the goal ahead.

Today I am setting my GPS for the goal

that I want as I listen to my intuition

guiding me only my highlighted route.

Affirmative Prayer Treatment 272

The past is over, the past is over, the past is over.

I will not look back at mistakes, loss and grievances

because I am focused on now and the journey ahead.

Ahead of me is the day I now choose as

I think about the kind of day I want to create.

I am in alignment with the Spiritual GPS that

God placed in me to guide me along

my happy highlighted route today.

Only good lies before me as

I follow my intuition and guidance today.

Affirmative Prayer Treatment 273

I do not have to be perfect, only willing.

I am more than willing to let Spirit guide and correct me

today as I walk in peace, joy and love.

I expect things to go well today and

I align myself with a day of Grace and ease.

My inner peace is unmoved by circumstances today.

I am centered in Truth and peace as

I open to receive the gifts the Universe has for me.

Wonderful things lie ahead of me today.

AFFIRMATIVE PRAYER TREATMENT 274

I am worthy and lovable because I exist.

I do not have to earn my place on the planet.

I do not have to justify my existence or worth

because I am a Divine Creation of the Great Spirit.

My talents and abilities are my happy contribution

to the world around me, but they are not planetary rent.

As a Child of God, I am under Grace and so

I am worthy and valuable simply because I exist.

There is no need to earn life by the sweat of my brow.

I joyfully contribute here because of my generous Spirit

and love & gratitude I feel for the Creator Who made me.

I am worthy and lovable because I exist.

AFFIRMATIVE PRAYER TREATMENT 275

I can let go of a story that does not serve me.

I would rather be emotionally biased and feel good,

than historically accurate and feel bad.

My life is not a press release of facts to be

studied and reported on like the evening news.

I can choose the stories to tell about my life

and I choose to tell the ones that feel GOOD

when I tell them, instead of focusing on unhappy facts.

I choose to focus on the positive aspects of my life and

to amplify them in order to feel good.

It is good to feel good.

I am choosing to feel good today.

AFFIRMATIVE PRAYER TREATMENT 276

I am no longer curious about things that will upset me.

I do not need to investigate and computer search

disturbing facts and news just because they happened.

Since I am under no laws but God's, there is

no need to terrify myself with what others are doing.

I do not need to know the latest family or work gossip.

I do not need to find more reasons to be upset.

Instead, I am investigating and very curious about

what is uplifting, life-affirming, creative and positive.

I am very curious to see how many miracles

I can experience this day, this week, this month, this year.

A<small>FFIRMATIVE</small> P<small>RAYER</small> T<small>REATMENT</small> 277

My life is not a popularity contest.

There are people who like me and those who don't.

That is none of my business.

I know that it is impossible to earn love or approval.

People love who they love – approve of who they choose.

It is my business to love and approve of myself.

I do my best and then let it go.

What others think of me is none of my business.

I know that I am a Child of God and

I am here for a happy Divine Purpose.

I am not here to please others.

I am here to please myself by

being Who and What God created me to be.

What others think or say about me is none of my business.

A<small>FFIRMATIVE</small> P<small>RAYER</small> T<small>REATMENT</small> 278

I am very slow to take offense and
very quick to forgive and let go.
I am not overly sensitive to what others say or do
because I am becoming more merciful and patient
with others and with myself.
Instead of wishing others would not push my buttons,
I am uninstalling those buttons more every day.
I am learning to let go of being offended and
I am dissolving my old defensiveness as
I choose to focus on mercy and forgiveness instead.
I am a work-in-progress, but
I am steadily moving forward as
I let Spirit heal my mind of taking offense.
I am in the process of becoming more
merciful and quick to forgive.

A<small>FFIRMATIVE</small> P<small>RAYER</small> T<small>REATMENT</small> 279

I am a vibrational match to joyous loving people today.

Today is a day of Divine Appointments in which

we all bring out the very best in one another.

Things move smoothly and effortlessly today

as we are all choreographed in perfect proximity

to others who are finding the good in Life.

We are all enriched today by moving in harmony

with this prosperous and happy Flow of good.

Wonderful things are happening today as

I am aligning myself with happy joyous people today.

Affirmative Prayer Treatment 280

People are happy to see me today.

I am a beacon of joy and Light today wherever I go,

even if I don't leave my home.

I am happy to see others today and

I recognize what is good about them as

we do the dance of Life together.

People are happy to see me today

and I am happy to see them.

Affirmative Prayer Treatment 281

I am seeing what I choose to see each day.

I see people doing a good job.

I see myself thriving and improving.

I see myself growing in wisdom and patience.

I see others doing the best they can.

I see beauty in nature.

I see order in the Universe.

I see opportunities expanding.

I see things improving in so many ways.

I see miracles and amazing transformations.

I see the good in the world.

I see good in others.

I see good in myself.

I am seeing what I choose to see today.

Affirmative Prayer Treatment 282

I am releasing the illusion of control.

I cannot control the world outside of me

or what others are doing or saying.

I can only guide my own emotions and perceptions.

I choose today to give up control so

that I can *positively influence* instead of manipulating.

I let go of resisting what is happening outside of me

so that I can be at peace and respond with wisdom.

I am relaxing into the flow of Life today

as I give up the struggle of trying to control the world.

AFFIRMATIVE PRAYER TREATMENT 283

I am forever connected to an Infinite Source

Which loves, guards and guides me every hour

of the day and night, every moment of my life.

With God, all things are possible for me

as I relax and let Spirit take the lead.

I surrender my self-will to the perfect joyous

Divine Will today, so that I may rest in God.

I am forever connected to my Divine Source.

AFFIRMATIVE PRAYER TREATMENT 284

My home is the Kingdom within me.

I can never be lost, never be away from home.

Everywhere I go is safe and holy ground because

my Home is the Divine Consciousness I forever dwell in.

Throughout the day I take time to be still and instant

and go Home again to the remembrance of

the glorious Kingdom that is my Divine Consciousness.

In any instant I can close my eyes, take a deep breath

and go to my Home within, where I am fed and restored.

AFFIRMATIVE PRAYER TREATMENT 285

The joy & peace within me can never be lost or taken away.

They were placed there by my Creator as eternal gifts.

This world didn't give them to me and so

the world can't take them away.

It is only possible for me to become distracted from them

as I tell myself terrifying or stressful stories,

but the joy and peace remain there waiting to be invoked.

I am invoking my eternal gifts of peace and joy today,

knowing that since the world didn't give them to me

the world can't take them away.

AFFIRMATIVE PRAYER TREATMENT 286

My goal is progress, not perfection.

Instead of looking at how far I have yet to go,

I focus on how far I have already come.

I may have backslid and fallen down a thousand times,

but I am only focusing on how many times I rise again.

I am continuing to go forward at my own pace

knowing there is no race, no competition, no prize to win.

I am making wonderful steady progress in

living in love, peace, joy and abundance.

AFFIRMATIVE PRAYER TREATMENT 287

I know that "lots can happen" when
I let go of trying to manipulate how my good will come.
This is an Intelligent Universe of limitless possibilities
and I do not have to design the formula for my success.
I trust that the Universe knows just how to
line me up with the answer to every challenge
and the open door to my greater good.
Instead of focusing on obstacles,
I focus on remembering that in this limitless Universe
of miraculous possibilities, lots can happen!

AFFIRMATIVE PRAYER TREATMENT 288

I am focusing on amplifying my strengths

instead of obsessing about my weaknesses.

Whatever God anoints me to do, I am well able to do.

I let go of comparing myself with what others

are anointed to do, or in envying their gifts and talents.

I have my own unique role to fulfill for which

I have been given gifts and talents.

I am focusing on tending to my own part of the Garden

and I know that each of us has a unique and important

role to play in fulfilling the joyous Will of God.

No role is more important than another.

The size of the role is irrelevant and meaningless.

We are all the multi-color threads in the Master Tapestry.

Each one is valuable and necessary to the Whole.

I am focusing on my strengths today as

I happily tend my part of the Garden.

A<small>FFIRMATIVE</small> P<small>RAYER</small> T<small>REATMENT</small> 289

I am quick to praise and point out the good

that I see in others instead of pointing out their errors.

I am quick to point out the good in myself

instead of pointing out and amplifying my errors.

I know that what I notice and take action on

will only grow and expand in my experience

so I am now choosing to praise and point out the good.

The good in my life is now growing and expanding

daily as I choose to praise and take action on

blessing and amplifying the good I see.

AFFIRMATIVE PRAYER TREATMENT 290

I am living in an Enchanted World of my own making.

I am creating my world by the thoughts I think

which are then projected outward creating my perceptions.

I choose to create a world of beauty and Light for myself

and for those who are in alignment with my world.

I relax my physical eyes so that I can see

with Spiritual Vision as my Enchanted World

of beauty, Light and Love arises before me today.

Affirmative Prayer Treatment 291

I am impervious and immune to the
limiting thoughts and beliefs of the
people and systems around me.
I am centered in Truth.

AFFIRMATIVE PRAYER TREATMENT 292

As I grow in physical maturity,

I am growing softer instead of harder.

I am expanding instead of contracting.

I know that loss is a part of physical life

and it can make me more fearful and small,

or it can make me more loving and oceanic.

It is my choice which way to go.

I am choosing love and expansion.

AFFIRMATIVE PRAYER TREATMENT 293

I am always healing in perfect timing and ways.

The Divine Intelligence which created me

set me up as a self-healing and renewing Being.

This Intelligence radiates through every cell

of my body as Divine Wisdom and harmony.

Therefore, I am always healing and restoring

without effort or struggle.

The more I relax and get out of the way,

the more efficiently and quickly I heal and renew.

I now relax and let my Inner Wisdom take over

as I remember that I am a self-healing Being.

When I see any healing or medical professional,

I know that they are using their skills to

compliment and assist my own self-healing.

Every hand that touches me is a healing hand.

Affirmative Prayer Treatment 294

Everything that needs to get done will get done

in perfect order and timing, in perfect ways.

The same Power and Presence that makes planets

revolve around the sun in perfect proximity

can run my life today and handle my projects.

I am a cooperative component with the Universal Source

in allowing the orchestration of magical manifestations

of joyously flowing accomplishment today.

I let go of worry, rushing and micromanagement today

so that I can witness how efficiently Source can do it all

through me and through all concerned.

I am a witness to the orderly efficient Universe today.

Affirmative Prayer Treatment 295

I am always at the right place at the right time.

Whenever I am ready to meet someone, there they are.

Whenever anyone is ready to meet me, there I am.

I trust my Source to work out all the details so

that I can relax and let the opportunity come

when it is ripe and ready for juicy picking.

My life runs in perfect timing and order.

When I am ready, the opportunity appears.

A<small>FFIRMATIVE</small> P<small>RAYER</small> T<small>REATMENT</small> 296

There is one Life, one Power, one Presence, one Source.

Whenever I am afraid or upset it is because I have believed

that there is a power or presence apart from God.

I remember now that there is nothing apart from God,

nothing to fear or resist or fight against.

I am standing in the Light which dissolves all darkness.

I AM the Light which dissolves all darkness

because He created me as the Light of the world.

Today, I am shining the Light for all those who

choose to remember there is only one Power and Presence.

AFFIRMATIVE PRAYER TREATMENT 297

I am not a victim of my past or present.

I am not a survivor of trauma.

I am a Child of the Infinite Living God of LIFE!

As such, I am a thriver and a miracle worker.

I release my past, present and future into

the Hands of God where all is blessed and healed.

Whatever horrors may have happened to me

are now being washed away by the Living Waters

of Divine Love and restoration.

I am now experiencing the healing of my mind,

and my Divine restoration to joy, sanity and inner peace.

I relax now and let this happen in perfect timing and ways.

I am thankful to God for this miracle.

I release it now for God to work out all the details

in wonderful ways for the highest good of all concerned.

And so it is. And so I let it be. Amen.

AFFIRMATIVE PRAYER TREATMENT 298

I am letting Spirit transform me as

all past grievances and resentments are dissolved

and removed from my consciousness.

With the Help of the Holy Spirit within me,

I let go of all past hurts and mistakes

even if they were just a moment ago.

I am a new creature in Christ as

I accept my Divine Inheritance as a Child of God.

I let myself be healed as by the Atonement (undoing)

as I focus my attention on this Holy Instant.

I allow miracles to undo all the effects of

errors from the past in the same way that

spring dissolves away winter from the world.

No matter my physical age, I am in the springtime of my life.

AFFIRMATIVE PRAYER TREATMENT 299

Since I have placed my future in the Hands of God,

it really is none of my business anymore.

I am under Divine Instruction and my life

is a work of art being continually created

by the Master Artist of all that is.

Whatever happens in my world today is under the

master tutelage and direction of the Master Hands.

I am curious and eager to see how it all joyously

unfolds in wonderful and surprising ways.

I am interested in living my life

as a creation of the Master Artist.

Affirmative Prayer Treatment 300

Wonderful joyous sums of money come to
me frequently for my personal use.
I am an abundant being with an unbreakable connection
to the limitless Source of all that is prosperous and good.
Whatever I need for my fullest expression of living
flows to me in steady streams of replenishing resources.
I am an open receptacle for the riches of God
and I always have enough to share and to spare.

Affirmative Prayer Treatment 301

I have never been rejected. I have only been spared.

When it seems I've been rejected it is only

because somehow it was not an energy match

with the person, place or situation.

We were being spared the pain of something

that was not right at the time for our greater good.

I know that I do not perceive my own best interests,

so I relax knowing that God's Plan includes all

that I need for my perfect happiness, in right timing,

in wonderful ways, with the ideal partners.

I rest knowing that Grace is guiding my life.

I release the past and know that

I have never been rejected, only spared.

AFFIRMATIVE PRAYER TREATMENT 302

My intuition is guiding me as the Universe

gives me all the right hunches to act upon.

I am becoming more in tune with Source Wisdom

and I know that I can trust my gut to lead me aright.

As I trust in Spirit-within to guide me,

confusion and worry dissolve.

I trust my Divine Intuition to lead

me to the open doors to my greater good.

AFFIRMATIVE PRAYER TREATMENT 303

My best years are still ahead of me.

I do not waste time ruminating on the past,

or worrying about the future.

I know that as I focus on the joy of this day,

my future is taking care of itself because

I am aligned with the Source of all Good.

Ahead of me is still great creativity, love, joy,

prosperity, interesting and loving relationships

with wonderful people, positive contributions

to the world and people around me and

wonderful new things to learn and master.

My best years are still ahead of me.

Affirmative Prayer Treatment 304

I am able to handle whatever comes along.

I always have whatever I need to handle

the challenges and situations of my life

because I know that God lives in me.

Of myself, I may be lost, beaten and confused,

but within me is the Presence which is forever

clear, strong, stable and wise.

I do not need to lean on my own limited human

understanding because I turn within to Source

to handle it all for me and through me.

If I am knocked to my knees by anything,

I stay there until I make contact with God's Grace

and I drink in that Love until I am able to rise again.

Within me is all I need to handle any challenge.

Affirmative Prayer Treatment 305

No one ever dies, we only change form.

No matter how many loved ones have gone on before me

we are only separate within the story of bodies.

I am forever joined with those I love as

I open my mind to make the connection.

I can feel the loving presence of those who have

made their transition to non-physical if I am

willing to not judge according to appearances.

Physical death of the body is not the end,

it is only a continuation of the spiritual journey.

I know that my journey is not over when I drop this body.

I will once again see my loved ones and we will

continue on in love together in God's perfect timing.

There is no death, only changes in form.

AFFIRMATIVE PRAYER TREATMENT 306

Everything I need to know is revealed to me today

in perfect timing and in perfect ways.

My good keeps emerging before me as

I learn to trust that Source is with me always.

I am never on my own. I am never alone.

I always have Help to Guide me and to reveal

to me how much I am loved and blessed.

I ask for and receive gifts from the Universe today

as I remember that I am a beloved Child of God.

I open to receive limitless blessings and Help today.

AFFIRMATIVE PRAYER TREATMENT 307

Life loves me and love pursues me.

I walk in perfect faith today that nothing can

withhold or deny my limitless blessings.

This is a friendly Universe which is always

giving me more of what I am focusing on.

I choose today to focus on the love given

and the love received as I walk the earth.

Everywhere I step is holy ground for

I am a favored Child of the Universe.

The right doors open and the wrong ones close.

This is a day of magical blessings and

delightful prosperous surprises and gifts.

AFFIRMATIVE PRAYER TREATMENT 308

I am always free to choose a new thought.

I do not have to believe everything I think.

If my thoughts are stressful or disturbing,

I can choose a thought with more breathing space.

I do not have to choose the most positive thought

anyone has ever thought in order to feel relief.

I can simply choose a slightly better thought as

I gently move myself up the emotional scale

one thought at a time.

I am always free to choose a new thought.

A<small>FFIRMATIVE</small> P<small>RAYER</small> T<small>REATMENT</small> 309

I select my thoughts as carefully as if

I were choosing a precious diamond at a jewelry store.

I do not treat my mind like a fast-food window anymore,

quickly grabbing something that will not truly nourish me.

Instead, I am choosing my own "pearl of great price"

each morning as my guiding thoughts for the day.

My mind is becoming a more beautiful place to dwell in

every day as I consciously select what I will place there.

I am designing a mental habitat that holds only

what is true, beautiful, holy, happy and life-affirming.

My mind is a beautiful joyous place to dwell.

AFFIRMATIVE PRAYER TREATMENT 310

I am not my mistakes, nor am I my past.

I am not defined by anything I do or have done.

God has defined me as a Divine Creation and

I only make mistakes when I forget that and

think of myself as a human body in a physical world.

I am a spiritual Being in a spiritual Universe.

I am remembering Who I am more every day.

The more I remember Who I am,

the more I am guided to act only from that awareness.

I am an eternal spiritual Being,

here only to joyously give and receive

the peace and blessings of God.

AFFIRMATIVE PRAYER TREATMENT 311

I am quick to praise and slow to point out errors.

I am learning to focus on what is right

instead of announcing what is wrong.

I know that encouragement makes things grow

and I am now choosing to focus on positive growth.

I am learning to appreciate what is, instead

of endlessly seeing what still isn't "perfect."

The more I praise, the more there is to praise.

The more I fix, the more there is to fix.

I am quick to praise and slow to point out errors.

Affirmative Prayer Treatment 312

I am enthusiastic about the road before me.

I have never lived this day before and

I am curious and delighted to see what

wonders Spirit has to show me.

I ask for and receive gifts from my Source today

as I open my arms wide to let in all the good!

I am a grateful gracious receiver.

Affirmative Prayer Treatment 313

I would rather heal than hold onto my story.

The basis of Consciousness is freedom to perceive.

I know that I am so free, I can even choose bondage

by holding onto a story of pain and loss.

I am choosing the freedom of healing as

I let go of any story that is not about

my Christic Nature lifting me up into

Grace, joy and the peace of God

that passes all understanding.

I am healed. I am whole.

AFFIRMATIVE PRAYER TREATMENT 314

I have decided to be happy today.

I have decided to focus on what there is to be grateful for

instead of what there is to be worried about.

I know that Christ Consciousness within me can

handle the details of any challenge in my life.

I choose to place it all in the Divine Hands now

as I focus my attention on gratitude and appreciation.

Thank You Spirit for the miracles before me today.

AFFIRMATIVE PRAYER TREATMENT 315

All things are held perfectly in the Hands of God.

I may not like what is happening at any given moment,

but if I judge not according to appearances,

I can return to peace and sanity remembering

that right here, right now,

all things are held perfectly in the Hands of God.

I am trusting in the loving Divine Mother-Father

to lead, guide and guard me today as

I cast my cares on God.

AFFIRMATIVE PRAYER TREATMENT 316

I don't know what anything means when
I am coming from my limited human perspective.
What I have considered loss has often been the
prelude to an upgrade from my Source.
Since I don't know that anything means,
I look to the Kingdom Within to heal my mind
and show me the right perspective to have
which will bring forth miracles and Light.
I am being shown the way to see
with true inner Vision instead of physical sight.
Today, I am seeing with true inner Vision.

AFFIRMATIVE PRAYER TREATMENT 317

I can always quickly return to my highlighted route.

It doesn't matter how far off-course I have gotten

or how long I have seemingly been lost,

my Source has never lost contact with me.

I simply remember how I want to FEEL

and I program that into my mind as I let

Source guide me back onto my joyous journey.

The Universe can bring to me the ESSENCE of

whatever desire I have as long as I let go

of my attachment to the form of things.

What is manifested is not as important as

how I feel at any given moment and

I am choosing how I want to feel today

as I open to receive the ESSENCE of my desire.

AFFIRMATIVE PRAYER TREATMENT 318

I would rather be happy than win a debate.

I would rather be peaceful than argue for my limitations.

I would rather feel love than hold onto being right.

I would rather prove God than prove my point.

I would rather sleep well than have the last word.

I am letting go of separation and attack thoughts.

I am letting go of guilt, shame and blame as

they are gently replaced by the peace and blessings of God.

Above all else, I want the peace and joy of God today.

I release all defensiveness as I relax into the

arms of the Divine Mother where I am

bathed in the healing waters of joy, love and peace.

I am choosing and accepting the peace of God today.

Affirmative Prayer Treatment 319

I am *letting* my dreams come true instead of

trying to force or manipulate them into being.

I know that I am not dealing with a resistant Universe

which I need to convince or petition for my good.

My Source has already given EVERYTHING to me

and my job is simply to align with it and let it in.

Each day I am opening more to let my dreams come true

in their *essence*, instead of being fixated on the forms.

As I relax and trust my Source, my good is often

very different than I pictured it, but *feels* even better.

I trust my Source as I am letting

my happy dreams come true.

Affirmative Prayer Treatment 320

I release my loved ones into Divine Care today.

I know that God's ministering Angels are tending to them.

I see them bathed in White Light and surrounded by Grace

knowing that they are held perfectly in the Hands of God.

I send them my unconditional love and acceptance

knowing that God is the Source of their good and

I am simply a vessel through which

that good sometimes flows.

I release my community, my country, this planet

into Divine Care today knowing that God's ministering

Angels are tending to us all.

AFFIRMATIVE PRAYER TREATMENT 321

Everything is lining up wonderfully for me today.

My connection to Source is growing stronger every day

and everything I need comes to me in perfect timing.

I align myself with God's Will each morning and

watch with wonder and delight as it unfolds before me.

I open to receive the Guidance and Love of my Source

and I share it with those who are open to receive it too.

Nothing good is withheld from me for

I am connected to an Infinite Source

Whose Will is my perfect complete happiness.

Affirmative Prayer Treatment 322

I live by Grace and not by works of the flesh.

I trust my Source to lead and Guide me where

I can be of the most joyful use and

receive the greatest blessings.

I am not living by wages or by earning my blessings;

my good is freely given by the One Who created me.

The flow of good is rhythmic and as balanced as breathing –

in and out, in and out, in and out – no struggle needed.

No worry, no stress, no competing.

I live by God's limitless Love and Grace.

Affirmative Prayer Treatment 323

I am growing in love and confidence every day.

I know that life is meant to be enjoyed and so

I allow myself to live the life I choose.

My Source is not withholding or judgmental.

There is no need for sacrifice or suffering in my world.

I am a beloved Child of God and

I am growing in love and confidence every day.

Affirmative Prayer Treatment 324

The more I enjoy my life, the more I prosper and thrive!

There is no value in being a victim or a martyr in my world.

The Kingdom within me is one of bounty and blessings!

My Source loves me beyond all reason and

I know it is God's good pleasure to give me the Kingdom.

I show my gratitude by receiving it with enthusiastic joy!

The more I enjoy my life, the more life there is to enjoy.

As I play and have fun, money pours into my accounts.

As I laugh and smile, love pours into my heart.

As I relax and rest, opportunities beat down my door.

My Kingdom is not like the human world of

scarcity and sacrifice and sorrow.

My Kingdom is one of ever-increasing blessings and joy!

AFFIRMATIVE PRAYER TREATMENT 325

I am writing the script of my life every day

through my thoughts, beliefs, expectations and focus.

I can write a depressing story, a horror story,

a melodrama, a romantic comedy,

or anything else my imagination can conjure.

I am the chooser of how I write the story of my day.

I now choose to write a story that I want to act out

with people who are fun to play with!

I savor playing my part today as

I write a wonderful story.

I am the producer, actor, director, author

and editor of my story.

I am writing a wonderful story for myself today.

Affirmative Prayer Treatment 326

I love and bless my body exactly as it is right now.

I release and dissolve any resistance or judgments

I may have about this wonderful body since

I know that it is a Divine Creation of the One Source.

It is the perfect size and shape for me today.

If there is any pain or discomfort in it,

I breathe in God's merciful kindness to that

part of it and I relax knowing that there is

nothing to get rid of, nothing to battle or fight.

My body is a precious gift and

I now choose to love and bless it just as it is.

I forgive myself if I have ever mistreated or abused it.

I forgive it for any judgments I have had against it.

I am now blessing my body and giving it to God

to joyfully manage and use for miracles.

I love and appreciate my beautiful body.

AFFIRMATIVE PRAYER TREATMENT 327

There is nothing to fear.

I know that my Guide walks with me and Guides me today.

Whatever happens, I am not alone and I have all the

Help I need to move through conditions in clarity and peace.

If I am afraid, it is only because I have forgotten my Guide

and am trusting in my own human strength instead of

leaning on the everlasting arms of my Christ Companion.

I let go of judging according to appearances as

I am now trusting in my Companion to walk me

through everything that comes my way today.

Affirmative Prayer Treatment 328

I am counting my blessings instead of counting my worries.

The vision of one world costs me the vision of the other.

Therefore, I am choosing to focus on the world of blessings.

It is up to me which direction I will look in –

the one of pain and sorrow, or the one of

miracles, love and limitless Light.

There is plenty of evidence for both worlds

but I cannot see both at the same time.

I am focusing on just how good I have it today.

I am focusing on how much more good is ahead.

I am counting my blessings today.

AFFIRMATIVE PRAYER TREATMENT 329

I am casting off guilt and shame today.

I am casting off worry and fear.

I am casting off self-criticism and punishment.

I am casting off attack and judgment.

I am casting off manipulation and control.

I am casting all my cares on God

knowing that God cares for me.

I am resting in God today

as I allow myself to feel good

right here, right now.

AFFIRMATIVE PRAYER TREATMENT 330

More each day I am remembering and accepting
my Divine Supernatural Nature as a Child of God.
I am allowing myself to be blessed beyond all past
precedent as I step into my Divine Inheritance today.
I boldly and fearlessly claim all that God has for me.
I humbly and gratefully share it with those God sends.
I am walking in love and gratitude today as
I allow myself to prosper and thrive
beyond all past precedent.
Wonderful magical things happen in my world
because I am remembering Who I am
and Who created me.

AFFIRMATIVE PRAYER TREATMENT 331

Wonderful synchronicity is happening more

frequently in my life all the time.

I seem to show up just when the good things

are starting and the right doors are opening for me.

The more I relax and enjoy my life,

the more these wonderful things happen.

I am not missing out on anything because where

I am is always the right place at the right time.

It's wonderful to watch how my life is choreographed

to meet up with so many wonderful experiences

and people as I simply tune into my own Guidance.

Affirmative Prayer Treatment 332

Each day I am relaxing more into the receptive mode.

At this moment, there is nothing to get, or fix or change.

Instead, I am opening to receive the gifts being given.

My heart and mind are receptive to the Divine Presence

and I am being healed, soothed and uplifted as

I align myself with the love, peace and joy of God

that is so freely and abundantly given me.

I am relaxing into the receptive mode.

A<small>FFIRMATIVE</small> P<small>RAYER</small> T<small>REATMENT</small> 333

I expect to have a wonderful day today.

I expect miracles to light my way.

I expect to be guided and led by Spirit.

I expect things to go well for me.

I expect love to flow to me and through me.

I expect to feel good in my body.

I expect to be inspired and guided.

I expect to receive gifts from my Source.

I expect to have wonderful interactions

with people in my world today.

I expect to be joyfully used by God to help.

I expect to prosper and thrive.

I expect a Divine Answer to any problem.

I expect things to unfold wonderfully before me.

I expect laughter and fun to flow.

I expect to have a wonderful day today.

AFFIRMATIVE PRAYER TREATMENT 334

It is easier and easier for me to see the good in people.

It is easier and easier for me to see the good in myself.

It is easier and easier for me to see the good in life.

I am appreciating life more each day as

I increase my focus on gratitude and appreciation.

As I shift my focus to the good,

the good offers itself to me at every turn.

There is a Divine Something that is responding to

my thoughts, attitudes and words.

The more I focus on the good,

the more good this Divine Something shows me.

A<small>FFIRMATIVE</small> P<small>RAYER</small> T<small>REATMENT</small> 335

I give myself permission to lovingly live as I choose.

I am not here to seek permission or approval from anyone.

I am here to express the One Life in my own unique way.

There is never a need to compare myself to another or

to what the culture says is "normal."

I wish no one any harm, and I do not want to control

other people or situations.

We are free to be who we are and

I am choosing to be exactly who I am

and to lovingly live as I choose.

As I give myself permission to live my life,

others are inspired to live their lives freely.

I am not fighting or pushing against anyone or anything.

I am simply lovingly walking my own unique path.

I give myself permission to lovingly live as I choose.

Affirmative Prayer Treatment 336

I have all the wonderful help I need.

I do not tell a "poor me" story because I know that

my Source gives me all the help I need if I will

simply align myself with the story of "blessed me" instead.

I am not afraid to ask for help and assistance.

I realize that people love to help and that

everyone is free to say "yes" or "no" without guilt.

I release everyone to do as they choose,

knowing that Spirit is bringing me into alignment

with all the right people and resources now.

I need not worry or scheme.

I have all the wonderful help I need

as I tell the story of "blessed blessed me!"

Affirmative Prayer Treatment 337

I stay in my own yard, in my own business.

There is never a need for me to "compare and despair"

over what anyone else is doing or not doing,

being or not being, having or not having.

We all have equal access to Source and have

our own part of the garden to tend.

No part is more important than another.

There is no need for anything but celebration

of the wonderful variety of ways to do life.

It is foolish for me to compare my interior life

to the exterior appearances of another's life.

I have no idea what another person is thinking or feeling.

I send everyone impersonal love and blessings

as I tend my own part of the garden today.

<u>Affirmative Prayer Treatment 338</u>

I prosper no matter what the current economic conditions

are or are not because of my limitless Source.

I am able to thrive and succeed no matter what is

happening in business, politics or the culture around me.

I have a wonderful innate knack for activating abundance.

I am always amply supplied no matter what

form the money or supply takes in the physical realm.

Abundance is forever flowing freely into my life

with enough surplus to share and to spare.

Whether my need is money, work, friends, love,

healing, ideas, opportunity, fun, homes,

or anything else, I tend to prosper and thrive

with a Divine Grace and ease.

AFFIRMATIVE PRAYER TREATMENT 339

I let Spirit work out the details of my good as

I focus my attention on the "what" instead of the "how."

How is not my part of the equation of accepting my good.

I choose the "what" of how I want to live and feel,

and allow my Source to work out all the details of how

it will happen in the physical realm.

I am on a "need-to-know basis" and

I am forever being joyfully guided down the

path to the essence of all that I desire.

I let Spirit work out the details of my greater good.

Affirmative Prayer Treatment 340

My body knows exactly what to do to bring itself

into alignment and balance no matter what the issue.

There is no such thing as impossible or incurable

for my Infinite Divine Source.

The same Power that Jesus used to heal the sick

and raise the dead is within every Child of God.

I turn to that Divine Physician within me and

allow It to restore me in perfect timing and ways.

My part is to relax and BELIEVE it is already happening.

I trust that my Source is healing my mind

and that my mind is healing my body.

I let go of time as I gently focus on

every tiny improvement as proof that

I am being healed and restored by Grace.

Affirmative Prayer Treatment 341

"Repent" means to "turn around."

I am able to turn around quickly anytime

I realize I am going in the wrong direction.

I do not need to feel guilty or punish myself.

I can make gentle correction and get going

in the loving, prosperous, healthy, happy

direction with ease.

I am able to change direction

anytime I find I have gotten off track.

Affirmative Prayer Treatment 342

I am able to speak my truth with ease.

I am not here to please others or to

bow to the pressure of the expectations of anyone

or anything outside of me.

My truth is *my* truth.

There is no value in me being phony or

in swallowing my true thoughts and feelings.

It is of no benefit to anyone for me to

hold myself down or to squelch who I am.

I am able to lovingly speak my truth with ease.

AFFIRMATIVE PRAYER TREATMENT 343

Loving myself allows me to prosper and grow.

As I give myself permission to love myself,

it inspires others to love and accept themselves.

I know that the way I treat myself is then

reflected back to me through others.

Other people will treat me the way I treat myself.

I am loving and respecting myself more than ever

and I see it reflected back to me as others do the same.

Affirmative Prayer Treatment 344

God Consciousness rules my world.

God is love and therefore so am I.

I now align myself with this Divine Love.

I allow this love to flow freely from me

out into the world around me.

I know that the way I know love,

the way that I feel love,

is by allowing Divine Love to flow through me

from the Kingdom within,

out into the world around me.

We are healed together in love today.

AFFIRMATIVE PRAYER TREATMENT 345

I treat myself as a valuable precious treasure.

I am as God created me and I am exactly

what I was meant to be.

There is a beautiful Light within me that holds and

protects me all through the day and night.

Nothing and no one can diminish this

perfect spirit that I am.

There are no words or actions from outside of me

that can change this beautiful beam of light which I am.

From this day on I will not harm myself in any way

in thoughts, words, or actions.

I treat myself as a valuable precious treasure.

AFFIRMATIVE PRAYER TREATMENT 346

I am surrounded by unseen angels who
love and watch over me.
They guide me to where I can do the most good
and where I can receive the most blessings.
I am a unique person in the Universe and no one
can take my place or fill the role I came to play.
I came to give and receive the peace & blessings of God.
I am lifted above the petty squabbles of the world as
Grace guides me in fulfilling my role of living from
my Center of Truth, love, kindness and mercy.
I am giving and receiving the blessings of God.

Affirmative Prayer Treatment 347

I release my family and loved ones into Divine Care.

They are blessed and embraced by Divine Love.

All their needs are taken care of this very day.

Their bodies and health are sustained by Source.

They are filled with vital energy.

Their finances come from Divine Supply.

They tap into the limitless Universal resources for

their abundant life, prosperity and happiness.

Joy fills their hearts and their minds are clear & calm.

They are safe from harm and free from fear.

Their good cannot be denied for it comes from God.

I forgive and release us from any past hurts.

We are encircled by the light of

deep forgiveness and acceptance.

We now step into a dynamic loving present

as we see one another in the Light of God's Love.

AFFIRMATIVE PRAYER TREATMENT 348

As I go to bed at night, I let go of the day behind me.

I deeply relax and let my body draw sustenance

from the Universal Source of Life.

My sleep is restful and healing.

My body and mind relax and let go.

My dreams are peaceful and nourishing

and I am guided by Angels to the Higher Realms.

As I sleep, my family and loved ones are

all held safely in the arms of God.

I am healing and renewing every night

as I sleep and rest in God.

AFFIRMATIVE PRAYER TREATMENT 349

All the brightest and best within me

is brought forward this day.

The Light of God shines brightly in me

and radiates out into all that I do or say.

My thoughts are high, my spirit soars,

and my heart is open wide.

I breathe deeply and release all tension.

Any anxiety dissolves into Divine Confidence.

I give this day to the Source of all good to control.

All outcomes are placed in the hands of

the perfect Love of God within me.

I am shining brightly today.

Affirmative Prayer Treatment 350

I am seeing things with miraculous perceptions today.

The peace of God is restoring me to peace, joy and sanity.

I call on and claim Divine Right Action

for all aspects of my day today.

God's Plan is one in which everyone wins.

I am invoking God's Plan now.

I slow down my thoughts.

I breathe deeply.

I relax.

I surrender to God.

I let go.

I am seeing with Spiritual Vision today.

A<small>FFIRMATIVE</small> P<small>RAYER</small> T<small>REATMENT</small> 351

I envision a world of love and harmony.

I know that all Life is cradled in God's loving arms.

Divine Love is now flowing through every country and

nation as every living being is embraced in peace.

There is no poverty, pain, sickness nor lack in God.

This is an abundant Universe and there are more

than enough resources for everyone to

have all that they need to thrive and grow.

Each person is now drawing to them all

that they need in order to be happy,

healthy, safe and loved.

Greed, addictions, anger, prejudice and sickness

all dissolve in the miracle of Divine Restoration.

The citizens and leaders of every nation are now

being awakened to the truth of our Oneness.

All beings everywhere are being lifted up

to their highest and best.

We recognize the sacredness of life.

We are all healed together.

We are joyfully used to shine the Light.

And so it is.

AFFIRMATIVE PRAYER TREATMENT 352

I invoke and awaken the Christ Consciousness within me.

I dip into the Divine Center of Infinite Supply.

Calmness, peace, clarity and tranquility are mine.

Nothing can move me from Center today.

Nothing can distract me from my loving focus.

Every breath I take renews my peace.

Every thought I think is guided by Source.

I am in alignment with Universal love and abundance.

I release myself and this day to the

all-loving Source to manifest miracles

in totally satisfying and delightful ways.

I am in alignment with Universal love and abundance.

AFFIRMATIVE PRAYER TREATMENT 353

I am releasing my thoughts of love into

the One Mind as a beacon of Light which

shines outward onto every street of the world

blanketing the world with God's love and safety.

We are healed together in this Light.

The family, tribe and nations,

whatever forms they take,

are restored by God's Love this very day.

Every school, park, playground, business and home

is protected and held perfectly in the hands of God.

The world is returned to sanity and peace

and I am seeing it happening now with

my inner Spiritual Vision.

I must see it first within and then

it can be manifested on the outer plane.

I am lighting up the world with Love today.

AFFIRMATIVE PRAYER TREATMENT 354

I now turn inward to the Center of my Being.

I go to the Well of Infinite Goodness and Wisdom

where I drink deeply from the Living Waters.

There is a perfect Presence within me which

now radiates love through my entire being.

I am at home here.

Calmness, peace and tranquility are mine.

The Father-Mother and I are One.

I am living from my Center today

as I drink deeply from the Divine Presence.

AFFIRMATIVE PRAYER TREATMENT 355

I am choosing to see God in all things today.

I now remember my Divine Self and

this reminds me of the Truth of all others as well.

Nothing and no one can separate us

from the infinite love of God.

There is no distance, no separation.

I am not alone, for God is with me now.

There is a Divine Plan for my life.

It is a Plan for my happiness and success.

It is a good plan and the one I want.

I joyfully surrender to the Divine Plan today as

I am choosing to see God in all things.

AFFIRMATIVE PRAYER TREATMENT 356

As an extension of the Creative Source of all Life

I am now going from success to greater success.

God is not a failure and as an extension

of God I cannot be anything but a glorious success.

I am stepping into my greatness and glory today

as radiant expression of the One Life.

It honors my Creator to allow myself to

prosper and thrive in this life.

Affirmative Prayer Treatment 357

I am finding my way more very day and

am being led by Source to all that is right for me.

I do not cling or hold onto anything for

by constantly opening my hands,

God is able to give me my daily good.

There is no need to "hoard manna" or any

form of good, for it all belongs to Source anyhow.

I am a vessel and a good steward of

the good that comes to me each day.

I let go of the old with grace when it is time,

and gratefully receive the new as it comes.

I am open to receive my good today.

Affirmative Prayer Treatment 358

I release and let go of what no longer serves me.

As I keep letting go of what doesn't work for me,

the only thing left is what does work.

My world is one of gentle contrast between

what is wanted and unwanted and

it helps me to sift and sort through life

so that can make wise and happy choices for myself.

Today, I am releasing what no longer works knowing

that I am creating space for more blessings to come to me.

I am gently letting go of what no longer works for me.

AFFIRMATIVE PRAYER TREATMENT 359

Divine Love, expressing through me,

now brings to me all that is necessary for

my highest and best good.

I am in alignment with the best of everything today.

I find something to praise and appreciate

everywhere I go today and in all that I see.

As I align myself with praise and appreciation

I draw to me endless blessings and miracles.

I am lining up with a day of limitless good.

Affirmative Prayer Treatment 360

I am telling my truth with love and clarity.

I do not have to argue or debate anyone.

I stand lovingly in my own truth and

do not need to defend or explain it

to those who would not understand.

I release others to stand in their truth

even when it does not align with my own.

We are all free to think and believe as we choose.

I do not need others to agree or approve

of how I choose to express or live my life.

I am telling my truth with love and clarity.

AFFIRMATIVE PRAYER TREATMENT 361

I am taking better care of myself all the time.

I know that there is no one coming to save me;

no one who has been put in charge of my good.

I'm the one. I must save myself.

I am saved from anxiety, stress and misery

by aligning myself with the Divine Source

and then taking action to treat myself

with loving-kindness and support.

I am responsible for me.

I am responsible for my happiness.

I am responsible for my thoughts.

I am choosing to put myself at the top of my list

for if I do not take care of myself,

I will not be of any use to anyone else.

There is nothing holy about depleting myself

or living like a beggar at the gate.

I am a Child of God and worthy of care.

I am taking better care of myself all the time.

AFFIRMATIVE PRAYER TREATMENT 362

I am authentically myself.

There is no one just like me.

I was created by Source as a unique individual.

I am a beautiful person, inside and out.

I am an instrument of Divine Love, healing & creativity.

I do not compare myself with anyone else.

I am not trying to fit in anywhere.

I draw to me those who appreciate me as I am.

I belong wherever I stand.

I have a right to exist.

I am authentically myself.

AFFIRMATIVE PRAYER TREATMENT 363

Age is nothing but a number.

I can start fresh even at 90 or 100 years young if I choose.

All things are possible in God and I live in God.

I can begin with tiny "penguin steps" to go

in the direction of any dream or goal I have.

Nothing is stopping me but a story in my head.

I am now telling a story of possibilities

and wonderful new doors opening for me.

I am an ageless spirit in a world

of limitless possibilities and miracles.

AFFIRMATIVE PRAYER TREATMENT 364

I open myself to this wonderful new day.

I do not know what is going to happen and so

I allow Divine Spirit to guide me and

to unfold all things in perfect order and timing.

Today I remember to praise and acknowledge

the people in my life with words & actions.

I am a grateful Child of God today.

Divine activity fills my day and runs my life.

I open my heart to give and receive love.

I open myself to this wonderful new day.

Affirmative Prayer Treatment 365

I am enough, just as I am.

I am not too much, nor to little.

I am wonderful, wonderful me!

I am focusing on what is really important today.

There is no need to strive for the myth of perfection.

It is okay if not everything gets done today.

The real perfection is not in outer accomplishments

or getting everything checked off a list.

Perfection is the eternal Light within us all.

I show up, prepared, on time, doing what I said

I would do, with a good attitude –

the rest is out of my control.

There is nothing I need do to deserve my good.

My worth is established by God, not by deeds.

I do my best, and forget the rest.

I am enough, just as I am.

NOTES

Jacob Glass is an author, spiritual teacher, mentor
and international supermodel. To order his other books,
see his live class schedule, watch online videos or receive his
weekly class recordings, see his website: jacobglass.com

Made in the USA
San Bernardino, CA
15 March 2018